Best Wishes

Legends in my Lunchtimes
by
Mike Newlin
ISBN: 978-1-9997646-1-6

Published by

i2i Publishing. Manchester
www.i2ipublishing.co.uk

Acknowledgements

I must make mention of the following:

The inspiration for this book came from a lifetime of memories of some of the greatest names in sporting history. Their stories entertained over a million guests at my business lunches. All these guests were also fed by an army of banqueting staff and chefs and we never knowingly poisoned anyone!

Many of the sporting celebrity speakers became my friends and I include many of them in my memoirs; not least, the 1974 British Lions Captain, Willie John McBride MBE who has kindly written the foreword. All the photographers in the book worked for me and I must thank them for enabling me to re-visit so many happy memories.

To my publisher Lionel Ross at I2I, your advice and encouragement was crucial.

My children and seven grandchildren insisted on a mention, they mean the world to me.

To Doreen, you are my best friend and rock, and occasional critic!

Finally, to my son Steve, without whom this book would never have been completed. My lack of computer skills is legend in the Newlin family, and Steve spent many hours and months preparing my manuscript for publication. But most of all his friendship kept me going.

*'**Legends in my lunchtimes**' is dedicated to him.*

Foreword by Willie John McBride, MBE.

It is a great pleasure for me to write a few words as a Foreword to Mike Newlin's book 'Legends in my Lunchtimes'.

I was first introduced to Mike by Gordon Brown of Scotland and Lions fame in the 1990's. Gordon at the time was one of the best speakers on the circuit, if not the best. After the first lunch at which I spoke for Mike as MBN Promotions, I can clearly recall realising, on my way back to Northern Ireland during the evening, that here was a man who ran a very professional event. Mike obviously cared deeply about his speakers and looked after their every need but he was also very aware of the needs of his clients and how they must have value for money. One of the best traits of his events was that money never changed hands or was mentioned at the time; this was all taken care of prior to lunches.

Mike arranged the lunches with special event themes. I recall, from a rugby point of view having reunion lunches of 1971 Lions and 1974 Lions. I think we had twelve lunches for each around the country - those lunches were great 'craic' and with stories from the past tours being greatly embellished. We also had a series of twelve lunches to select the Greatest Lions Team of all time. These lunches caused a great stir among our audiences.

Personally, I had a super series of events around the UK speaking with my old friend and adversary Colin Meads of All Black fame. Terrific memories of speaking and meeting some of my heroes from other sports over the years and being met time and again by Barry – Mike's driver at various airports. Mike thank you for such wonderful memories and well done in giving us, your speakers, such a platform to tell our stories. You are missed terribly from the entertainment scene. Good wishes for your book which I know will give a lot of enjoyment to so many people.

Willie John McBride

Introduction

Life Before MBN

I always suspected that I would be an event organiser. In my teens, I was aware that I would not be a top sportsman, I loved many different sports/games – football, golf, cricket, tennis, table tennis, squash … I could play quite well, but I knew 'quite' was not enough, so I gravitated to coaching and as part of running a football club, I had to raise the funds to hire grounds, and deal with kit. I persuaded Mum and Dad to wash the muddy outfits every week and I even got Doreen (who was my girlfriend at the time) to embroider the club badges on our first set of shirts. These were bought from Romford manager Ted Ditchburn's sports shop. Ted, an ex-Spurs and England goalkeeper, had tried (with little success) to coach me, but it was always good to speak to the great man.

My star signing for Arroway Athletic was Gerry Cronin. In the early days, we were discussing the future of our team in his bedroom in Hainault, when his dad called out that there was someone to see him. It was the Chelsea manager, Tommy Docherty, who spent half an hour trying to persuade Gerry to play for Chelsea, but Gerry turned him down – can you believe it? I asked him why he didn't want to go to Stamford Bridge, and he finally told me that he supported Fulham and his hero was the great Johnny Haynes, so he couldn't play for their local rivals! He did go briefly to Leyton Orient, but he loved his Sunday football for Arroway, and played more than three hundred games over the years.

Even in the sixties and seventies we needed to raise lots of cash and I ran a stag night – I was amazed how much it generated. I'm sure that the 200+ guests were there to listen to the comedians; the scantily clad young ladies had nothing to do with it …

My life needed an income and I worked for the Halifax Building Society, where I met Doreen, and later the now-defunct

Northern Rock Building Society, where I progressed very quickly to become a branch manager. Having married Doreen in 1970, and started our family of four (Sarah, Theresa, Lisa and Stephen), I still knew that I would do something for myself in the event organisation world. My first toe in the water was getting to know the Surrey and England spin bowler Pat Pocock, and helping in a very small way with his testimonial year. At Northern Rock in Croydon, I also met a well-known photographer who specialised in theatre called Frazer Ashford. I organised some exhibitions in Croydon and at our head office in Newcastle, and through Frazer I met James Aubrey, who was a big star in *Bouquet of Barbed Wire* on television, and also Connie Booth, who had co-written *Fawlty Towers* with her then husband John Cleese. We had a party in the office for the cast of the Tennessee Williams play *The Glass Menagerie*, starring James and Connie.

Completing the cast for the *Glass Menagerie* at the Ashcroft Theatre were Angus MacInness, who had been in the film *Rollerball*, and another star of stage and screen, Maxine Audley. As I was getting them their drinks I discovered that Maxine had brought a friend along with her, he was a friendly soul, and when I asked him what he wanted to drink, I also asked his name. 'Call me Charlie,' he smiled, so I did and everybody laughed – especially when I handed him the drink with a cheery, 'Here you are Charlie.' I found out from Jimmy Aubrey that my new friend was Sir Charles Groves, one of our most famous conductors for many august orchestras including the Royal Philharmonic! But it was a good party and I thought that I liked this world.

Soon after I arranged a small sponsorship for the Royal Philharmonic Orchestra, and whilst classical music was not my thing, I got to know the lead horn player, John Bimson, and put on a lunch in Croydon at which John said he would come and speak. What a good lad he was and some of his stories made me change my view of classical music; they seemed to have more fun than footballers! It was at that lunch that the seed for MBN

Promotions was sown. Pat Pocock was to be the next speaker but fate took a hand and my bosses at Northern Rock asked me to manage the Manchester office. My move north put an end to the Croydon project. The idea was still in my head, though, and our Monday trips to Manchester's famous Brahms and Liszt pub were the catalyst that started me off on organising sporting lunches for the business community.

Back in Hainault in the early sixties, I had tried another pastime when I joined Hanwell Productions, an am-dram group led by Barry Rowlandson, brother of my best friend Ian. Now Barry must have had really good taste as he cast me as leading man in a number of productions. I was the Reverend Lionel Toop in *See How They Run*, a Philip King farce, and also Mitch Mitchem in *The Long and the Short and the Tall*. Another farce, *Simple Spymen*, followed and I was Simon Sparrow in *Doctor in the House*. It was, however, in a murder mystery called *Murder without Crime* that I finally crashed. Ian Rowlandson was to play the lead, but got very early stage fright (not on stage, but in rehearsals!) and Barry came to me and asked me to step in. It was a four-person play, and I had to learn a large and complicated script – my co-star was a new girl to the team – Linda Cecil, and I had to stab her to death in the first act. Her character, Grena, was a vamp, and during rehearsals I was using a real Bowie knife that Doreen had brought me home from a holiday. We wrestled in the rehearsal and the knife slipped down Grena's front and she let out a yell informing me that, 'You've stabbed my breast!' She showed me the offending wound – she was amply bosomed as the saying goes. However, my girlfriend Doreen, who was helping out at the company, was not impressed by my viewing Linda's figure and for many (many) years if the plays were discussed, Linda was 'That Grena girl ...'

Football, cricket, drama and courting, I really don't know where I found any time to work! I would have gone on the stage if truth be told, and I did have a chance to become an assistant stage manager at the Stratford Little Theatre (run by Joan

Plowright) but £3 a week, with no certainty that I would be the next matinée idol, put me off the idea.

Chapter 1

MBN

MBN Promotions started in 1980 to provide sporting celebrity lunches for the corporate entertainment market. Lunchtimes worked – it was the right atmosphere to do business, and I've worked out that over the years we've entertained over a million guests. I hope many of them will have fond memories of the events – everyone got to listen to and many got to meet their sporting heroes in person, I wonder how many autographs were signed over the years – and I'm sure most of them were treasured and are preserved still in offices and homes across the country. The events had a lovely atmosphere, and we had a lot of fun – sometimes at a guest's expense … I remember one particular lunch, at the Manchester Piccadilly in the 1990s, where there was an issue with one of the guests' cars blocking the car park exit. The hotel staff asked if we could request its removal – so I asked the audience 'Could the owner of a car with the registration number XX please move it to allow access.' The owner stood up and headed through the tables to the foyer – as he was doing so I followed this up with 'Yes, these brown Skodas always get in the way,' causing a huge laugh in the room. This was in the days when Skodas were very cheap and had a famously bad reputation, although I don't think the owner found it as funny as we did as he slunk out to move his beautiful Bentley.

We also saw how technology changed over the years – when I started, mobile phones simply did not exist, but as they quickly became an essential of the modern businessperson, there were many occasions when they went off mid-speech, and it would drive certain speakers to distraction. To try and combat silly ringtones going off during a speech, I started some lunches with a little housekeeping – 'We've agreed to do some specialist market research for Vodaphone, if you have a mobile phone on you, would you get it out, and wave it above your head please. Well done – now turn it off!'

We are social creatures and, despite the rise of smart phones, virtual offices, Skype and social media, we still do our best business face to face in the company of our peers – I don't think that will ever change, the power of networking can never be underestimated, and that's why the lunches and sporting dinners still continue to be popular to this day.

When I sold out to Nigel Wray, the owner of Saracens Rugby Club, in 2006 the publisher Harper Collins contacted me. I had cooperated with journalist Tim Collings to produce a successful book for them for the millennium called *Reuters' Century of Great British Sport*. They now suggested that an account including the famous (and occasionally infamous) characters who had featured at my sporting lunches over the previous twenty-five years would make a very good book.

When it became clear that they were particularly interested in some of the more risqué stories that involved my events and theatre nights with George Best, I decided that I did not want to do that. My memories of working with the greatest names who have graced sport over the past fifty years have given me so much pleasure, there's a thousand happier sporting stories that should be retold and remembered.

So why now produce a memoir? Well many of my most famous sporting characters have passed on, others are getting longer in the tooth and some of the younger ones have gone on to fame and fortune. What draws them all together is that brilliant ability to make me, and thousands of people, laugh. Is there a better medicine??

I hope you will enjoy my trip down memory lane, but do remember, these are *my* memories.

Chapter 2

George Best

Left to Right – Rodney Marsh, Mary Shatila, Mike Newlin, George Best and Wilf McGuinness. Taken at the Hotel Piccadilly, Manchester.

Many people thought that they could analyse Bestie. Why did he not play longer for Manchester United? Why did he only date three Miss Worlds? Why did he drink so much? Well that question has never been answered – everybody has a theory – some may have got close to the truth but thousands did not. I would never claim to have a definitive view. What I can say is that George was great box office for me and my events. We did many lunches, some with Denis Law, others with Rodney Marsh, including a brilliant theatre tour with Rodney, Peter Brackley and Mike Osman. It was not until he was in the Badlands of his drinks problem that George ever missed an event. Sadly, that occasion was a 'Memories of Sir Matt Busby' lunch in Manchester, and by then he was on a slippery slope that was to take him to dark places.

When it was his turn to speak he would start with 'Hands up everyone who thought that I wouldn't turn up?' and then 'I am currently writing my autobiography, can anyone tell me where I have been for the past twenty years?'

He also talked of the famous incident in Birmingham when dating Miss World, Eva Rueber Staier. Having dined, they went to a casino and won twenty grand in cash. When they got back to the hotel it was very late and they were let in by the night porter, an Irishman from Belfast, who obviously absolutely loved meeting Bestie. George asked him if he would get a bottle of champagne and bring it up to his room. A short while later 'Paddy' arrived with a bottle of Bollinger … and three glasses! He had just put the tray in the room when Eva came out of the bathroom in a negligee that left little to the imagination. Paddy saw the money that George had thrown on the bed, and came out with the classic … 'Mr Best, where did it all go so wrong?!'

George would also say when asked where all the money he had made had gone, 'I spent 50 per cent on drink, 40 per cent on gambling and blondes, and just wasted the rest'

We once spent a great day with George's son Calum on a trip to Yeovil, where George was to open a new stand at Yeovil Town's ground. Calum was only in his early teens and he and I went and had a kickabout on the pitch, while George did the honours for the club. On the way back to London, Calum fell asleep and George suggested we have a football quiz to pass the time. Now I thought my football knowledge was good, but Bestie was in another class altogether. We battled and argued all the way to Chelsea (where George lived then). I'd like to think it was a draw, but I also found out later that George had an IQ that would have qualified him for Mensa.

One of our theatre nights was in Jersey in the Channel Islands. Mary Shatila, George's girlfriend and minder at that time, came with us. It was a good night and I got out the three bottles of champers that the pools company Vernons gave us for every night on tour. Rodney Marsh, Peter Brackley, Mike Osman and Mary drank very little so George polished off most of the three bottles, and added some Moët to the bill to boot. Next morning, we all pitched up for breakfast, minus GB. However, to our surprise, he soon appeared, bright as a button, into a crowded hotel breakfast room. Many eyes were on him as always, when a waiter arrived at our table with a teapot and cups on a tray, which he put before George, who poured himself a cup and drank it down. You could see the guests smiling. I leaned over and saw it was not Darjeeling but chardonnay.

In May 1993 George, Denis Law and I met up at Manchester Airport for the short flight to the Belfast City Airport, now of course renamed the George Best Airport. We were flying the night before an MBN lunch planned for the following day at the famous Europa Hotel in Belfast city centre. As we approached Belfast we flew over Strangford Lough and it became very misty. It seemed that the descent into the runway was taking a very long time. Now Denis is not a happy flyer and, as time passed, he became very unsettled. As the airport finally came into view we were quite low, so low in fact that the engines roared and we pulled up fast, only just (or so it felt at the time) missing the Harland and Wolff crane that sits in the dock where the *Titanic* was built. The intercom crackled into life and the Irish captain came on with these exact words: 'Sorry about that folks, I missed the runway, I'll go around once more but if we miss again I'll take you to Belfast International at Aldergrove ...'

'F****** hell' was all that Denis, or indeed anyone on board said. Denis put his head in his hands. However, thankfully for us, lap two saw a perfect landing and earned the pilot a relieved round of applause, even from the Lawman.

You have to bear in mind that 1993 was in the middle of the 'Troubles', and the Europa Hotel resembled Fort Knox when we arrived, but an excellent dinner, a good night's sleep to calm the

Lawman's frayed nerves, and a superb MBN lunch made it all worthwhile. Dickie Best, George's dad, came along and it was a pleasure to have him there. Also joining us on the day was Jim Boyce, Chairman of the Irish FA (who went on to be Vice-President of FIFA), who was an old friend of mine and Bestie's. We flew home with no problems, but that night the IRA blew up the Opera House next to the Europa, (that by the way was the most bombed hotel in the world – thirty-two times). The lorry packed with explosives ended up in the hotel restaurant, where we had been dining the night before. Damage was in the millions but what would have been the story if they had killed George and Denis?

Chapter 3

Sir Stanley Matthews

Left to right - Wilf Mannion, Sir Stanley Matthews, Duncan Mckenzie and Mike Newlin. Taken at the Forte Crest Hotel, Newcastle. Wilf was Stan's great friend from the England team in the late 1940's.

Could you ever find two outstanding footballers like George Best and Stan Matthews who were so far apart?

I first met Sir Stan, then just Stan, at the Hotel Piccadilly in Manchester, home of my lunches in the early days of the 1980s, prior to MBN Promotions expanding throughout the UK. Over 400 guests came to hear the great man speak. Bear in mind that though he was seventy at the time, he had only been retired from First Division football for twenty years. He was still playing for Stoke City at the age of fifty, something that will never happen again.

The closest I came to seeing him play was in the 1962–3 season when Stoke came to Brisbane Road for a Division One evening game against Leyton Orient. It was the O's only season in the top league, and I watched a lot of their games. A capacity crowd of probably 17,000 were packed in, all coming to see the great Stanley Matthews. At 7.15 the loudspeakers announced that Stan was injured and could not play. I can still hear the sound of the whole crowd sighing in disappointment. We got a glimpse of him in the dugout, but that was the only time I saw him in the flesh. So, when he arrived at the hotel I was nervous, to say the least.

I remember asking him if he had really been injured for the Orient game twenty years before. 'Certainly, I had a bad knee and failed a fitness test,' was Stan's reply. I was so relieved as I'd feared at the time that it had been a ploy by Orient to boost the gate numbers – Stan put thousands on the attendances at every game Stoke played home and away. I realised he was not a natural event speaker, but after the lunch finished he stayed for well over an hour signing autographs and some posters his agent had brought. Gordon Taylor (CEO of the Professional Footballers' Association) still has the signed poster on his office wall in Manchester. I went home happy, and was back to work on the following week when my wife Doreen phoned to tell me that a large box had arrived by courier. Just in case it was a bomb she decided not to open it. When I got home we bravely opened the box, and inside was a lovely Staffordshire china teaset from Stan, with a card to say thanks for looking after him. It was the first of many happy events and acts of friendship and kindness which carried on until he died in 2000.

Stan would not dwell on the famous FA Cup Final in 1953, although it had become known as the Matthews Final for his incredible performance in the 4–3 win over Bolton Wanderers at Wembley Stadium. Stan was over forty then and people were saying he would never get an FA Cup winners' medal. However, he proved them wrong and the win was applauded around the world. Typically, Stan told us that it should have been called the 'Mortensen Final' as his great Blackpool friend and teammate Stan Mortensen scored a hat trick to secure the win. I asked Stan Mortensen at a lunch whether he agreed with Stan about the 'Mortensen Final' comment – 'I certainly do' was his honest (if tongue in cheek reply).

I think modestly that I helped Sir Stan tighten up his speeches. In the early events, he would tell a story about meeting the Great Train Robber Ronnie Biggs in Brazil whilst he was on a coaching tour. Whilst this was totally factual I was never comfortable with a story that glorified an on-the-run criminal, and I sensed that many in the audience felt the same. So (with some trepidation) before a lunch in Colchester, one of our smaller occasions, I suggested that the Biggs story was not popular and perhaps he should leave it out? He gave me a look that filled me with terror, but smiled and agreed. His speech earned Stan a standing ovation, which was not unusual, but I also felt I had done well. He never used the story again in my company.

At the end of the Second World War the great Russian team Moscow Dynamo were invited to play in four 'friendlies' – one each in Glasgow and Cardiff, and two in London, at Chelsea and against Arsenal. Stan was invited to guest for Arsenal. They played at White Hart Lane (Tottenham's ground, as Highbury was out of action) on 21 November 1945. Almost 60,000 turned up to see the great Dynamo, but London gave them a traditional pea-souper fog that day and the game was in serious doubt. However, the Russian referee (no neutrals in those days if you can imagine that now!) said he could see the goals from the half-way line and the match was on. As the game progressed the Dynamo goalkeeper annoyed Arsenal by taking ages to clear the ball from his area and constantly bouncing it, as you could do in those days. At half time Reg Drury told his team mates, that he was fed up with the goalie and would barge him if he didn't clear the ball quicker. In the second half Drury was true to his word, and despite the worsening fog was seen by the referee and promptly sent off ...

Bernard Joy the Arsenal captain asked Stan to drop into right-half to cover for Drury, which Stan did. Five minutes later Stan got a call: 'Stanley go back on your wing – I have returned!' It was Reg. He had sneaked back in the fog and played the rest of the game! It was found out later that Moscow Dynamo had played with twelve men for twenty minutes, so honours were even. Arsenal lost 4–3.

Stan went on to say that years later he was coaching in Rhodesia, now Zimbabwe, when he was introduced to Rhodesian Prime Minister Ian Smith. 'I saw you play,' the Prime Minister told Stan. 'When was that?' asked Stan. '1945 for Arsenal against Moscow Dynamo.' Ian Smith had been a fighter pilot in the war and had been at White Hart Lane. Stan wondered how much of the game Smith could have seen in the fog, but he said he was delighted to have been there.

My best friend on the circuit was the wonderful British Lions and Scotland second-row forward Gordon Brown – you will hear a lot more about Broon frae Troon later in the book, but on one occasion he did speak with Sir Stan at a lunch in Glasgow. 'The Broons' were a tremendous sporting family and Jock Brown, Gordon's dad, had been a soccer keeper with Partick Thistle. He had also represented the Scottish League versus the English League on 3 November 1938 at Wolves' Molineux ground. The *Scotsman* newspaper said goalkeeper Brown was the team's hero for his performance. Back at the lunch Broonie was recounting the story to Stan, when the great man told him that he remembered the game very well. 'I had beaten three men and ran into the box and unleashed a shot, getting ready to celebrate a goal, when the Scottish keeper pulled off the best save I had ever seen.' After the lunch Broonie rushed home to see his dad and tell him what Sir Stan had said. Jock, who by the by way was a tough character, and in later life physio to the Scottish rugby team, was very moved, and wished that his brothers Jim and

Tom (both former professionals) had been there to hear what the great Stanley Matthews had said about him.

I was preparing for an MBN lunch at Chester with Stan, when he called me to ask if he could bring a friend to the event. I was delighted and I asked Stan who he wanted to invite. Stan advised me it was Jackie Mudie. Jack, of course, was another member of Blackpool's famous 1953 side, and was a Scottish international forward. Stan went on to say that Jackie lived in Stoke (where they had played together after leaving Blackpool) but was having difficulty with finances (top division players in the 1950s were not paid like today's stars; his maximum wage was only £20 a week throughout his career). Stan went on to ask if I would take a couple of hundred pounds out of his fee and slip it to Jackie for attending. There was no way I would ever have reduced Stan's fee, and I was delighted to have Jackie at the events. What a lovely man he was, and proved very popular with the guests. He came to a number of lunches after that and was always great company. As Jack got older he became quite ill, and was eventually admitted to Stoke Infirmary. Stan called to ask if I would go to see Jackie in hospital, so we met up and were joined by another ex-Stoke player, who was more famous for his days at Wolves and England – Eddie Clamp. Eddie was one of the game's hard men and 'looked after' Stan when they played together. Stan recalled a game he thought was at Oldham Athletic when a nasty full back booted Stan so hard that he ended up on the shale area off the pitch – he picked himself up and limped back onto the park to hear the dulcet West Midlands voice of Eddie 'Don't worry Stanley I'll do him.' And he did! We three arrived at Jackie's bed to find that he was obviously very poorly, but seeing his mates and me perked him up considerably. Just to listen to those three old internationals talk football was a joy; just that they included me in the conversation was a privilege. I did of course make them aware of my own goalkeeping skills, which prompted much laughter. We laughed for over an hour until Matron threw us out for disrupting the smooth running of Stoke Infirmary.

Shortly afterwards Stan phoned to say that the tough little Scot had scored his last goal. Not many will know that Stan had helped raise money from the PFA to help his pal out, something that Stan had also done for Neil Franklin, the former Stoke and England centre half, who sadly developed Alzheimer's in later life. Some people used to say that Sir Stanley Matthews was careful with his money – I sure hope he was because he was a generous friend and certainly helped me progress my business.

Stan was always asking me to go to a match at the old Victoria Ground in Stoke when I did not have a game at the club I was involved with, Altrincham. I took my son Stephen along one Saturday. We picked Stan up and took him to the ground. We were shown to a hospitality box and joined by Stan's brother. Stan took Steve, whom he had never met, to meet the manager and players and even offered him a trial when he was older (he was fourteen at the time). Steve politely declined, probably a good decision! The following week a letter arrived for Steve from Stan, enclosing some coaching lapel badges from Africa and Brazil. Every time I spoke to Stan, he always asked how Stephen was getting on, and to say hello from his pal Stan.

In February 1995, I helped celebrate his eightieth birthday at a lunch at the Grosvenor House in London's Park Lane. Guest speakers were Sir Tom Finney and Nat Lofthouse, with comedy from Jackie Blanchflower – Danny's brother and himself a Busby Babe who survived the Munich air disaster but never played again. What a great speaker he was – but much more about Jackie and Sir Tom in later chapters.

One of my last requests of Stan was to pay a visit to Altrincham. I had set up the youth team for the Conference side, and organised a tournament for local schools, the final to be played at our Moss Lane ground. I arranged for Stan to come and give out the medals. As he shook each lad by the hand I'm not sure if they had any idea who the elderly gentleman in a baseball cap was, but their dads certainly did! A footnote was that the referee was a very young Anthony Taylor, now one of the top Premier League officials. I don't know if it was Anthony's first 'major' final, but he certainly impressed Sir Stanley Matthews.

I last spoke to Stan just before Christmas in 1999. I wanted him to do an event but he said he was off to Cyprus to stay with a pal and get some sun on his old bones. In early February, I had not heard from him so I rang Stoke City and they said they were worried as he had not been in touch. He got home from his trip, but fell ill and died in North Staffordshire Hospital on 23 February 2000. I could not attend the funeral as I was hosting a lunch in Bristol (I think he would have approved) and that day we toasted one of the greatest sportsmen of all time.

25

Chapter 4

Broon frae Troon

Left to right – Kevin Connelly, Gordon Brown and Wilf McGuinness. These were three of my favourite speakers from my 10th Anniversary of MBN tour in 1990.

My first meeting with Gordon Brown was at a lunch at the Hotel Piccadilly in Manchester. He was a branch manager with the Bristol & West building society in Glasgow. When he arrived, he said that he had played a bit of rugby! Just imagine this giant in full Scottish kilt, 6 feet 5 and maybe a stone (or two) over his playing weight of 17 stones. With a charming smile, he quickly won over the Mancunian audience.

'I come from Troon in Scotland, and I'm from a very sporting family. My dad Jock played football, the round ball kind, for Scotland and became physio to the Scottish rugby team. My mum was a star hockey player and my brother P. C. Brown famously captained the Scotland rugby team, when we stuffed the English. Then there's my sister – she's game for anything!'

After lunch, he confided that he did not have a sister …

I was in the early stages of building MBN and I did not see him for a couple of years, but we kept in touch as we had got on so well from day one. However, as my number of venues increased, I was able to use him more and more.

His stories were often naughty, but always hilarious … 'As a building society manager, I used to call on a solicitor's office in Falkirk to do some business. They had two receptionists who showed me the difference between the cities of Edinburgh and Glasgow. Elizabeth was from Edinburgh and wee Betty was from Glasgow. One Monday Elizabeth came in to work and over coffee said, "Do you know Betty I went to a marvellous party at the weekend, after twenty minutes I lost my knickers." Betty looked shocked, "What? Knickers, to a party?!"'

Broonie continued on the cultural differences by telling us that he had been in a Glasgow cinema, when the girl in the row behind shouted, 'Hey you! Get your hand out of my pants … Not you … you!' This was also the time when Glasgow was nominated as European City of Culture, which he said came as a very big surprise, mainly to folks who came from Glasgow.

By 1994 Gordon had become one of my best friends, and everyone at MBN loved the big man. We even discussed the possibility of him joining the organisation, but Broonie loved the speaking circuit and by that stage was doing 150 events a year throughout the world, so we carried on with the lunches, and I got him a number of engagements with other organisers. A good part of Broonie's speech featured his role in the greatest British Lions tours of all time to New Zealand in 1971 and South Africa in 1974. So popular were his tales that I suggested we should do a series of events.

So 'The Boys of 74' was born. Broonie introduced me to the legendary captain of the South African tour – Willie John McBride, who lives in Ballyclare in Northern Ireland, and he flew over for the first of our lunches, in the Queen's Hotel in Leeds. We were joined by a new speaker who had been one of the stars in '74, Phil Bennett, and over coffee I asked Broonie how we should play the speaking. We agreed that as the new boy 'Bennie' would go first, then I said Willie John would go second. Gordon just smiled and said, 'No. I will go second.' I argued that this was unfair and that Broonie as the star turn should go last. We did not agree but as he was much bigger than me I accepted very reluctantly. Well, nigh on 500 guests were there, and I did not enjoy my lunch. Brown had spoilt it for me. However, as a good pro, I introduced Phil Bennett, who did speak superbly. I then had to get up and introduce my ex-friend Brown, who did his twenty minutes and as you can guess got a standing ovation! I rose to introduce Willie John, and as I sat down I whispered, 'Bastard' in Broonie's ear. McBride rose to a standing ovation and thrilled the crowd with as good a speech as I could ever recall. He finished to another 'standing'. More of W. J. McBride later …

Gordon Brown became the only British Lion to play in all three tours in the 1970s, and is still regarded by many as Scotland's best second-row forward of all time.

In 1971 Broonie linked up in New Zealand with the man soon to be a close friend, Willie John. During that winning tour over the All Blacks, Broonie was rooming with Willie John when W.

J.'s great friend and second-row partner, Delme Thomas from Wales, got injured and Broonie was picked to make his Lions debut alongside his roommate. On the afternoon before the great day, Broonie plucked up the courage to ask the Irish legend (then on his fourth Lions tour) whether he thought Gordon was up to the job. Without looking up from his newspaper, he puffed on his pipe and said, 'I know who I would prefer.'

Broonie must have done well, and by 1974 he was number one choice to partner Willie John, by now the captain of the Lions. It was the time of apartheid and many in the UK, including the Prime Minister, did not want the Lions to go to South Africa. The squad met up in a Hyde Park Lane Hotel and were faced with many protestors. Broonie said that the Wales hooker Bobby Windsor wanted to go outside and fight them, as he loved a good punch up!

Willie John got all thirty players into a meeting and told them, 'You know there are many who think we should not go on this tour. If anybody here wants to pull out they can leave now, and no one will think any less of them.' Not a soul moved. The tour was on and it turned out to be the greatest tour in Lions history, before or since.

Broonie's stories from the tour were many and a lot included Willie John. My favourite featured a giant Springbok forward, Johan de Bruyn, selected for the Third Test of that series to cause mayhem amongst a Lions side that were beating all before them. Broonie told of de Bruyn's size – enormous – and that he only had one eye, earning him the nickname 'Cyclops' (but never to his face)! At a ruck early in the game, someone bumped 'Cyclops' on the back of the head and out popped his false eye. Broonie then went on, 'You now had the most amazing scene on a rugby pitch where there were thirty players on their knees saying things like "Where were you Johan when you lost your eye?" Someone found his eye and handed it back, and de Bruyn, without ceremony, stuffed it back in the socket – we all looked amazed as there was a great lump of grass sticking out of the socket. We ran over to the next lineout, and Willie John said to me "Broonie, I dare you to pull out that f****** lump of grass."'

Broonie said of the call of '99' by Willie John that the skipper had introduced it to stop the thuggery going on from the Springboks. His words were simple 'When I call '99' you hit the nearest f***** to you.' Broonie said he was aghast, he came from Troon, 'We don't do that sort of thing.' Nevertheless, when the call came, Broonie waded in, just watch one of the clips of the match on YouTube! It sorted out all the problems, and the call was not needed often. Broonie, though, said that there was another occasion when the boys were getting an ice cream in Johannesburg and Willie John asked for a '99' in his cone and all hell let loose, blood and vanilla ice cream everywhere!

My Christmas lunches at cities across the UK were a massive part of MBN, and each year I had to come up with new ideas. So, 1999 saw me bring Broonie together with Wilf McGuinness, the former Manchester United manager, and Kevin Connelly the impressionist from the *Dead Ringers* radio and TV show. Our three speakers tried to outdo each other for the three weeks we were on the road together, and as a consequence they became not only rivals, but firm friends.

It was during this 'tour' that we began to worry about Broonie. We had a full-time driver, Barry Dickinson, with us and following a lunch in Nottingham we were to go on to the Manchester event the next day. We were going to deposit Kevin and Gordon in the hotel. Broonie, however, asked us to drop him at a hotel in Hyde in east Manchester. He got some stick from the car as to who the lucky lady was, but no, he was going to do a dinner engagement, he was not feeling great, and when Barry said he would pick him up late that evening Gordon did not argue. He was brilliant in Manchester the next day but I was concerned. It turned out to be the beginning of a long fight against that dreaded disease, non-Hodgkins lymphoma.

We spoke most weeks while he underwent chemotherapy and, during a period of remission, I organized a 'Scottish Speaker of the Year' lunch in Glasgow. Four speakers competed; BBC TV commentator Dougie Donnelly; Ron Yeats, the famous Liverpool FC and Scotland centre half (who hailed from Aberdeen); Sandy Jones, the Chief Executive of the Professional Golfers' Association; and, as bald as a coot, but ever smiling, Broon frae Troon. I don't think I have to tell you who won the trophy. He was thrilled and the other speakers voted for him as well!

Later in 2000 I phoned and asked how he felt. 'To be honest, Mike,' he said, he felt like 'shit' and every bone ached. However, he and his wife Linda got away for a break in Spain, and he sent me a postcard full of optimism to say he was on the mend. Sadly, it was not the case and the cancer took hold again.

In March 2001, his friends organised a dinner at the Grosvenor House in London. Gordon invited me to sit on his table on a night when over a thousand people, including most of rugby union's greats, were in attendance. 'Cyclops' Johan de Bruyn flew over from South Africa, Johan spoke little English, but when he was introduced to the audience, Broonie's face was a picture! The big Afrikaner got up on stage, got out a present of a glass eye on a plinth to give to Gordon, and proceeded to get a sheet of foolscap to read. 'Broonie, the wife and me love you,' and went back to his table. He summed up what everyone privileged to be there that Wednesday night was feeling. On that Friday, I was back at the Grosvenor House for a lunch that I had originally planned for Broonie to address, but I'd changed it as the big man was too ill.

To my surprise the first person I walked into at about 7.30 in the morning was Broonie's brother Peter. He saw my surprised look and told me that Gordon was still at the hotel – they had looked after him as he was too unwell to go home. Peter said they were getting a taxi to take him to the Brompton Hospital in Chelsea. I said that Barry would take him in our people carrier, it would be more comfortable. Peter went up and got Broonie. He was in a wheelchair, and laughed when he saw me. I gave him a kiss and said 'Goodbye Broonie.' He smiled that famous smile. 'Au revoir not goodbye,' was all he said …

Gordon Lamont Brown died on 18 March 2001 in the Ayrshire Hospice at the age of fifty-three.

Even at the funeral in his beloved Troon he got the last laugh on some of his rugby pals. Amongst the pall-bearers were former Lions and England captains Bill Beaumont, Roger Uttley and Fran Cotton. Billy Beaumont confided to me that Broonie's coffin weighed such an immense amount that it felt like it had solid lead in it. Bill said he had recently had a knee op, so was cursing Broonie all the way to the car. At the cemetery, a lone piper played a lament as we said goodbye to a great pal who loved making people laugh.

When both Peter and Gordon were playing for Scotland in the early seventies the rivalry between them came to a head when P. C. was out of the side, but the talk in the press was that the Brown brothers might be in the second row together. Broonie was in his office during the week before the selection when he got a call from his brother. 'Gordon, great news, I'm back in the team.' 'Well done, but who's been left out?' was Broonie's reaction. 'You have,' was P. C.'s reply …

Gordon said Peter was always jealous because Broonie was bigger than his elder brother. Peter used to complain that their mum always gave Gordon more potatoes. One day the boys asked her why she only had the three boys? She told them that every fourth child born in the world was born Chinese, 'And I'm not cooking rice for one!'

Gordon played his club rugby for West of Scotland and there was only one game that none of the players liked to play in. This was a visit to the Scottish Border town of Langholm. 'I'll tell you what it was like in Langholm – they eat their young!' On one occasion the West of Scotland scrum-half got the ball from a scrum, thought he saw a gap and nipped down the blindside where he ran into the Langholm flanker, who flattened the number 9 with a warning to follow, 'Come down the blindside again and I'll f****** kill you.'

The offended man appealed to the international referee Alan Hosie, 'Mr Hosie, did you hear that?' 'I did,' was the referee's reply. 'Well, what are you going to do about it?' 'I'm doing nothing, but I suggest that you should go on the open side next time!'

In 1970 the Scottish Rugby Union celebrated its centenary year and the centenary game was to be against England at Murrayfield. What was unusual was that it was to be played the Saturday after Scotland had met England at Twickenham in the Five Nations. During that game Broonie had what in polite circles was called an altercation with the England lock Nigel Horton. Put more simply he belted Nigel at a line out. Horton was hurt but sought retribution. This did not happen but at full time he caught up with Gordon with the famous words, 'Brown, next Saturday at Murrayfield, I will f****** kill you.' Broonie said that the English Rugby Union saved his life because they dropped Horton for that match.

Chapter 5

F. S. Trueman

F.S. Trueman and Sir Tom Finney. Taken at Chester Racecourse at Fred's request, as Sir Tom was his footballing hero.

Left to Right - Brian Statham, F.S. Trueman, John Conteh and Sir Peter O'Toole. Taken at Fred's 65th birthday party at the Hilton Hotel in London.

I first met Frederick Sewards Trueman at a charity dinner I organised for the Round Table in Brentwood in 1970. Fred had not long been retired from cricket and was making a reputation as a comedian. I got his telephone number from a newspaper reporter, and he readily agreed to come along. The fee was agreed, and he asked for a hotel room and a bottle of Scotch, again all agreed. Now reading this today you will not believe that in those days it was quite common for strippers to be invited to dinners. The Chairman ordered it, so who was I to argue? I booked a charming young lady from Basildon, and having got Freddie sorted with his room, I had to find our lady friend somewhere to 'change'. She asked the format for the evening and I told her that she would perform before our guest speaker. On being told that the speaker was Fred Trueman she got quite excited as Fred was her hero and could I organise an autograph for her? I said I was sure Fred would oblige. Her exotic dance went very well, and as she finished (completely starkers) she came up to top table and asked F. S. for his autograph. I did wonder where she kept her autograph book! She just smiled and got Freddie to sign her bottom! As I paid her after the event she said she would not wash again, and was Fred staying the night? 'No,' I said, he was driving back to Yorkshire. I told Fred that I had saved his honour but I won't reveal what he called me …

As the years went by Fred spoke at every one of my MBN venues, some on several occasions. In this chapter I will concentrate on stories that he told, and later I will tell about the tours we did together with 'From the Commentary Box' when he stepped in to replace the late, great Brian Johnston. He also joined me on luncheon tours with Sir Garry Sobers and another with Frank 'Typhoon' Tyson.

Some people would tell me that F. S. was an old curmudgeon, always moaning – but not to me, he was one of my best friends and if ever any speaker had to drop out, even if it was on the day of the lunch, Fred would always stand in, often driving many miles to get there. I particularly remember him driving to Manchester at the crack of dawn to catch a flight with me to a lunch in Exeter. To my horror the flight was cancelled, but he would not hear of letting the guests down. So, I phoned the hotel to get the room ready – luckily our sponsor was a good pal called Mike Allison, who said he could start the lunch off if we did not get there by 12.45. So, I drove like a bat out of hell, and we just made it. F. S. spoke superbly, and we drove back to Manchester Airport so he could drive home to Yorkshire, probably getting there well after midnight. Did he moan? Not a word; and he rang me the next morning to see if *I* was alright!

Fred was a cricket historian in his own right – he collected books on the game and they gave him a lot of stories that he used to great advantage during his speeches. He was not always politically correct but, as he would say at the end of his speeches, 'I hope I haven't upset anybody today, but If I have I don't give a bugger!'

He talked of touring India for the first (and probably only) time. 'That food caused me trouble, even if you had a cast iron stomach that food would go through it! It was a fortnight after I got home before I could break wind with any confidence. I kept my cheeks so tight together that you couldn't have got a tram ticket up there.'

What did annoy him was when people would ask him if he did actually say to the Indian High Commissioner at a dinner in the West Indies, 'Pass the salt, Gunga Din.' He swore that he was not guilty m'Lord. He did get fined £100 on that tour, but Fred said that it was because the Reverend David Sheppard, later to become Bishop of Liverpool, let a slip catch go through his legs for four runs. 'Sorry, Fred, should have kept my legs closed,' was David's shout. Fred replied 'Not you, David, it's your mother should have kept her legs closed.'

Bill Shankly claimed he said the same thing to goalkeeper Tommy Lawrence, the 'flying pig' as Tommy Smith called him, when a goal went through Lawrence's legs, but F. S. maintained, 'I said it first and it cost me money!'

Fred recalled a match in the 1930s (quick to add not a tour he was playing on) when the Duke of Norfolk's XI played an Indian side in Delhi. The tourists were to bowl first, and several players were under the weather. The 'Delhi belly' had struck the night before. Alf Gover from Surrey was asked to take the new ball. The umpire called 'Play' and Gover raced in to bowl the first ball. But when he reached the crease he just kept running, past the startled opener, between the wicket-keeper and slips and up the pavilion steps. The captain, Douglas Jardine, went to see what had happened to him. When he got in the dressing room he called out, 'Gover, where are you?' 'In the toilet, sir, I have shit myself.' 'Well can we have the ball back? We need to start the game!'

Alec Skelding was also a fast bowler, who played for Leicestershire in the early twentieth century. He had a benefit year in 1927. Fred said he got about £50 and put the lot on a horse running at Sandown Park. It lost, and the Leicester committee offered him another benefit, which he turned down. 'I can't afford it,' he told them. So, Alec turned to umpiring, and became a very popular character. Fred told of a game on a very windy day, the batsman, Fred said it was Geoffrey Boycott (but I do wonder if it really was), missed a ball that kissed the off stump, and a bail fell off. Somehow no one appealed, so 'Geoffrey' picked up the bail and replaced it, looked at Alec and said, 'Windy today, Alec.' 'Aye it is. Mind it doesn't blow your hat off on the way back to the pavilion ...'

Frank Tyson was one of the fastest bowlers of all time. Fred said he was one of the few players to terrify him. When the 'Typhoon' as he was nicknamed retired, he became a teacher in Melbourne, Australia, and was a respected radio commentator over many years in Oz. Fred asked if I might be interested in doing some lunches with Frank, when he visited the UK. At the events F. S. told a story from 1954, when Tyson's Northants side visited Taunton to play Somerset.

The Somerset captain was Ben Brocklehurst, one of the last amateur skippers in the county game and later owner of the *Wisden* cricket yearbook. Ben won the toss and decided to have a bat. Just before the start a very sharp shower blew over the wicket and, as the pitches were uncovered at that time, the Somerset openers were subject to a physical assault by Frank Tyson, resulting in two players being conveyed to the local hospital. Ben Brocklehurst would normally not be expecting to bat so early, but as the wickets fell, Ben was seen to leave his captain's room and head into the player's dressing room. He was seen to wrap towels round his thighs, then put in his 'box' protector, and then a wicket-keeper's protector as well. He put a bath towel round his chest, and towels around each forearm, pulling on a long-sleeved sweater and batting gloves, pads and cap – no helmets in those days. A wicket fell and, looking like the Michelin man, he was heard to mutter, 'That bastard Tyson is not going to hurt me.'

He took guard. Tyson raced in and bowled a yorker that broke
Ben's big toe!

William 'Hopper' Levett was one of Kent's wicket-keepers in
the 1930s. Hopper was an amateur and played in the county side
when Leslie Ames was on test duty. Now F. S. said that Hopper
did rather enjoy a libation, more than most by all accounts. One
morning when Kent were playing Middlesex at Canterbury the
dressing room door opened and in staggered Hopper, still in
evening dress from the night before. As he was the only wicket-
keeper on the staff, and paid his own expenses, the decision was
taken that he should play. The players got him into his whites
and keeper's gear as Middlesex were batting first. They poured
a gallon of black coffee into the poor man and the umpires stuck
their heads into the room. 'Ready to play, gentlemen?'
'Certainly,' came the reply and the Kent side took the field, with
a player either side of Hopper, holding him by the pockets and
squatting him down, where they thought a keeper should squat
to receive the ball from a fast bowler. 'Play!' and the opening
bowler ran in. The Middlesex opener shouldered arms outside
the off stump and the ball whistled past Hopper's right ear. He
never moved – four byes. The second ball went the same way,
eight for no wicket. 'We could lose this game on extras,' was the
slips' view. The third ball pitched leg stump and the opener
glanced it towards fine leg, only for Hopper to dive full length
and catch the ball inches off the ground. Hopper got up, tossed
the ball to the slips and remarked, 'Do you know that's the first
time I've caught someone off the first ball of the match.'

Fred was not always a respecter of 'toffs'. An amateur captain
(not Ben Brocklehurst!) came out to bat for Cambridge
University, in all the latest gear of the time, best calfskin pads
and gloves and so on and a pristine bat that had never been hit.
He also spoke to the Yorkshire team with comments like, 'Lovely
day. Have a good game.' Fred was not impressed. He did not
'sledge' opponents. He just ran up and removed the batter's
middle stump. As he walked off he said to F. S., 'Good ball,

Trueman.' Fred responded, 'Aye, wasn't worth getting dressed up for, was it?'

Fred had much to remember about Frank Tyson, not least one painful memory. Yorkshire were playing Northants and Tyson was bowling particularly quickly. Going out to bat to face a second new ball was Yorkshire and England's left arm spinner Johnny Wardle. As F. S. was next man in, he watched with more than normal interest. Wardle saw a delivery from Tyson whizz past his nose, and as the 'Typhoon' raced in for the next delivery Johnny backed away to square leg and the ball removed the middle stump, passing (as Fred said) the toe of Wardle's bat – at full stretch!

'As Wardle made his way back to the pavilion I put down my pipe and as he came in to the dressing room I said what sort of a shot was that? And went out hoping the fast bowlers' union would save me from a battering.' Fred took guard, and Tyson bowled a straight delivery that F. S. patted back – the second ball was also blocked. However, the third ball was a bit shorter and Fred saw it early. 'I thought, help yourself Fred lad, and I played a great pull shot … before the ball arrived, I felt it when it arrived … I was hit in what Johnners would call the nether regions. As I collapsed in great pain the Northants team all gathered round. Why does everyone laugh when someone gets hit in the box? Got out my protector – it was split in half – and it took several minutes before I was able to carry on.' Fred did not last much longer and Tyson ended his misery by knocking out all three. Fred made his way back to the dressing room where Johnny Wardle was doubled up laughing. 'What sort of a shot was that?' he asked. 'I slipped in the pile of crap you left out there,' was Fred's curt reply.

One lunch I wanted to do, but never managed was F. S. and Geoffrey Boycott. I knew both men well so I asked Fred why he had fallen out so badly with 'Boycs'? 'There's no problem,' was his obviously untrue answer. So, I threw the same question to Geoffrey and got a similar response. A change of tack was needed. Fred loved the money so I suggested that there could be thirty or forty grand each if the two Yorkshire legends would do all my events. That hit the mark and Fred phoned Geoffrey and told him of my idea, and Geoff said he would think about it. So, phase two, I acted as go-between and the famous meeting to heal many years of hurt was arranged. The venue was to be Headingley, on the first day of a test match. The day came and the meeting took place behind the *Test Match Special* commentary box and the television box, where Geoffrey was to work.

Then the muck hit the fan. Fred thought it would be a good idea if Boycs and he got together to save Yorkshire cricket (which was in a poor state at the time) so Fred planned a double-page article to appear in the *Sunday People*, which Fred wrote for, on the next Sunday. A photographer was there to record the occasion. Geoffrey went potty, all deals were off, and I never got my star lunches, although both men continued to work for me individually. Geoff was very angry that Fred had already told his newspaper that he and Geoff were going to 'save Yorkshire CC' when he hadn't asked Geoff about this first!

Our story did not end there. A few years later Geoffrey phoned to tell me that he had throat cancer, it was serious and as you can imagine even one of our greatest batsmen realised that this was an innings that would need his very best resolve. I rang Fred – he was very upset and to my surprise, when Geoff rang me, he told me that F. S. had been in touch, and they kept in touch. Thankfully Geoffrey made a brilliant recovery.

Geoff and Fred finally buried the hatchet, and not in each other!

In 2006, the greatest fast bowler of all time, by his own and many others' judgement, was struck down by the dreaded lung cancer. He probably did his last engagement for me. My great friend Melvyn Letts, who sponsored many of our lunches, was opening a new office in Milton Keynes, and I asked Fred to do the honours. I did not know how ill he was, but as ever he agreed. Could he go by train, he asked? 'Of course.' So, he went to

Peterborough from Leeds, with a suitcase full of his autobiographies. Melvyn picked him up and F. S. kept him entertained all the way to the office and then back to Peterborough, minus the books that Melvyn had purchased for his clients. It could have been his last deal as Fred's wife Veronica phoned several days later to tell me that Fred was in the Airedale Hospital and the prognosis was bad.

Frederick Sewards Trueman died on 1 July 2006. He was the first England cricketer to take 300 wickets in the world, he got an OBE and he gave much entertainment at my events for over twenty-five years.

Fred's 'Retirement' Dinner

Fred asked me if, as he reached retirement age on 6 February 1996, I would consider running a celebration dinner to mark the occasion. I quickly got to work and accountant David Nesbitt said he would like to sponsor the event, which I planned at the Hilton on Park Lane in London. Guests from many big companies signed up to come. Fred was delighted, and we then considered who to invite among his friends and sporting colleagues. Fred said that I ought to invite Prime Minister John Major, a big cricket fan. Fred said it might help him get his knighthood! I think he was joking! I telephoned Number 10, and was put through to the PM's Principal Private Secretary, who said that the PM would be asked. The following day they came back with a Yes – he would be thrilled to attend. There were a few protocol rules. Firstly, I had to be positively vetted (no problem I'm pleased to say). Next, apart from Freddie, no one had to be aware that the PM would be in attendance. It was a sensitive time politically. Thirdly, the PM's personal protection officer would be at the Hilton to make sure all was in order, and finally the police sniffer dogs would check every nook and cranny. It was my job to meet the PM when he arrived at the hotel. After an introduction, I led him upstairs to take him to the 'green room'. Now I knew the Grosvenor House up the road like the back of my hand, but not the Hilton, so I managed to take the

PM up a long corridor to a dead end! Luckily everyone laughed (except me), and we finally got to the sponsors' room. What a sight! There were about thirty famous faces standing in a line, all signing cricket bats provided by Reg Simpson of Gunn & Moore. Fred thought they would raise a pile of cash for his hospital charity. F. S. saw the PM and came over and they had a chat. I looked down the line of celebrities – Peter O'Toole, Ted Dexter, Peter Alliss, Farokh Engineer, Brian Close, Jeffrey Archer, John Conteh, Rory Bremner – and the list went on. Dinner was about to be called and Fred said, 'Ask the PM if he will sign the bats.' 'You've got to be kidding,' was my reply, but he was not, and muggins went to the PM with Fred's request. 'Certainly, delighted,' came the response and he did!

As I was hosting the event, I sat next to the PM and a few seats away was Jeffrey (now Lord Archer) who kept a conversation going with John Major. He kept telling me to call the PM 'boss'. I should coco, no way was I addressing the Prime Minister as 'boss'! However, the PM nudged me and whispered, 'Please call me John.' He was great company, and thoroughly enjoyed the night. I think I gave him one of the signed bats (at a very reasonable price).

Rory Bremner was a superb speaker, and his John Major impression went down a storm.

Jeffrey Archer had phoned me a few weeks before the dinner. Could I help with the speech he was to make on the night. I suggested that Don Mosey, the 'Alderman' as Johnners called him in the *Test Match Special* box, would have some good stories about Fred. Great idea said the noble Lord – Don was not well enough to attend but wrote a superb speech that Jeffrey delivered quite brilliantly, to a huge ovation. Don never got a thank you, and I'm still waiting – a bottle of Scotch would have gone down well!

In 2001 I was having lunch at Fred's house in Flasby, near Gargrave in the Dales, that Fred and Veronica had come to love. Well after retiring as a player, Fred would turn out for the village team. Fred started to show me his cricketing memorabilia, and asked the best way to sell some of it. At the time, I was considering linking up with Chris Cowdrey and an auction company, GR8S. They got excited by the idea of auctioning Fred's famous collection, and did so. I'm still waiting for my bottle of Scotch from that introduction as well – I was obviously not the best negotiator. I am not sure how much was raised at auction but Fred seemed happy and later asked me to help Trevor Bailey auction his memorabilia.

Chapter 6

Our 'Enry

Left to Right - John Conteh, Mike Newlin and Sir Henry Cooper. Henry is wearing his Variety Club blazer, he raised thousands of pounds for them over the years.

I first met Henry Cooper in 1982, before he became Sir Henry (it was an honour he was very proud of). Our 'Enry as he was often called was without doubt one of the nicest men I ever had the privilege to know. Henry spoke at most of my venues over the years, and he had a kind word or autograph for everyone he met. I particularly remember once when I was setting up for an MBN lunch in Exeter (Henry was driving down from Kent) I popped out to the hotel lounge for a coffee and walked into the famous ice skater Christopher Dean, who was waiting for Jayne Torvill to arrive, as they were doing a show in Devon that night. He asked what was going on as there was a buzz around the Rougemont Hotel, and I said that Henry was speaking at a lunch.

He was a hero of Christopher's so I asked him if he wanted to meet Henry when he arrived. He joined us for a pre-lunch drink, though he wasn't able to stay for the lunch itself. As he left he thanked me and said it had made his day. Henry had that effect on literally thousands of people, including my wife!

We were on a 'tour' of lunches, and travelling from one in Glasgow to go on to Manchester, where Henry was booked in to the Hotel Piccadilly. I suggested that he come home with me to have dinner with the family. 'Yes please,' was his response. Doreen went potty when I told her Henry was coming to dinner. 'What in God's name do I cook for Henry Cooper?' She decided on spaghetti bolognese, and nearly had a heart attack when she found out that Henry's wife Albina was Italian. She need not have worried. Henry licked his plate clean and his compliments meant that he replaced Stan Matthews as her favourite!

Henry was a South London boy, brought up near the Elephant and Castle. His grandfather was a tough character, who had been a bare-knuckle fighter in his early years. As granddad got older he went to live in the flats that formed part of the Peabody Estate at the Elephant and Castle. He told of arriving home on his landing, where a neighbour who had just returned from the pub was beating his wife. Granddad weighed in to protect the woman and hit the neighbour and, as they fought, the woman took out a long hairpin and stuck it in granddad's backside, pinning the cheeks of his rear end together. He had to sleep on his stomach for several days and told Henry never to get involved in family arguments.

Henry was an identical twin, and he and brother George turned professional together, under the management of a larger than life character, Jim Wickes. To celebrate turning pro, Jim took the twins to a nice restaurant 'up West' in London, and after lunch Henry took Jim home in his new car. Not a Rolls Royce yet! Jim squeezed in the back as he was about 18 stone, and George and Henry sat in the front. It was belting down with rain, and as they reached Jim's road Henry saw a cyclist battling the elements. 'I thought I could get past him, and pull up at Jim's house. But as I drove past the cyclist I went through on enormous puddle and the poor bloke got soaked. He was not pleased and banged on the car window. I thought I had better get out and calm him down. I got out and George and Jim did as well. Now I was about 13 stone, and 6 feet, George was a bit heavier, and Jim Wickes was about 18 stone. The cyclist was not young, very thin and about 7 stone wet through, and he stood between us three as we got ready to apologise – 'I suppose you think you're bleeding brave, the three of you?' was the surprising remark from the cyclist.

As Henry progressed he got to fight and beat many great heavyweights, but everyone remembers the famous fight with Cassius Clay, later to become Muhammad Ali, in 1963. At the end of round three, Henry hit Clay with a left hook that floored the great man, and only the bell (and some nifty work in the corner) saved him from being beaten. He recovered to beat Henry but years later, on Michael Parkinson's chat show, he said, 'The punch that Cooper hit me with, did not just shake me but shook my relatives in Africa.' Henry went on to fight Ali again in 1966, when a bad cut to Henry's eye saw the end of the fight. Henry had a lot of trouble with bad cuts, and finally finished his career with a much-disputed defeat to Joe Bugner – many pundits thought Henry won that fight, including Henry! Our 'Enry as he was known throughout the UK never forgave the referee, Harry Gibbs. Conspiracy theories abounded, but Henry accepted the decision and moved on in his life to become a national treasure.

The only time I feared for the life of one of my speakers was when the BBC commentator Garry Richardson at my lunch in Newcastle said to Henry, 'If you had not been cut so often in fights, do you think you would have been knocked out a lot more?' Henry's smile was perhaps a tad icy on that occasion!

Henry loved his golf and raised many thousands for his charities, but his proudest time was when he was elected president of the Grand Order of Water Rats. Some of the great names in show business were 'Water Rats' and for a boxer to become King Rat said much for the regard they had for 'Our 'Enry'. Henry remembered that members who had to miss a lodge meeting would send their apologies. His favourite apology was a letter from that great comedian Les Dawson. It went, 'Dear King Rat Henry, I'm sorry to miss the meeting, but unfortunately my cleaning lady has had a bad accident. We found her at the top of the stairs in the foetal position, with the hose of the hoover embedded in her rectal area. However, I can report that she is picking up nicely again!'

One of Henry's boxing pals, who also went on to become an actor after retiring from the ring, was Nosher Powell. When that famous American world champion Joe Louis made a tour of the UK in the 1950s, he needed a sparring partner, and Nosher's manager offered him the job. Three rounds of sparring at a tenner a round was a fortune in those days, so Nosher jumped at the chance. Being a cool customer Nosher knocked on Louis's dressing room and introduced himself, 'Hello Joe, I'm Nosher Powell and I'm going to spar with you today. Do you mind not hitting me on the head, as I'm getting married soon, and I don't want to upset my girl?' 'No problem, I'll just hit you on the arms,' was Joe's response. Brilliant thought Nosher, thirty quid and no cuts. What he didn't know was that Louis fought fighters at exhibitions in the States, for what was called 'Bum of the Month', and he would just hit their biceps, until they couldn't lift their arms. Then he would knock them out! Nosher went in the ring and wallop, Joe belted him on the arms for three rounds. Nosher got home in agony – and he was booked for the following day as well. Next morning he knocked on Joe's door again, 'Hey Joe, do me a favour, just hit me on the f****** head will yer ...'

Henry always finished his speech with a letter he received from a woman who had been given a new radio by the Variety Club Golfers' Society: -

'Dear Mr Cooper,

Thank you for the lovely new radio. When my old radio broke down I asked my neighbour if I could listen to hers, as I did not have a television. She said no and I was quite upset. However, when my lovely new radio arrived I was thrilled and my neighbour asked if she could come in and listen – I told her to f*** off.'

51

Chapter 7

Jack Charlton

Left to Right – Geoff Miller, Martin Bayfield, Mike Newlin, Jack Charlton and Denis Taylor. Taken at the Grosvenor House, London at one of our Sporting Speaker of the Year lunches.

It's 8 June 2015, and I am watching the television to see a friendly international in Dublin between the Republic of Ireland and England. At the last meeting of the two countries, in 1995, the Ireland manager was Jack Charlton. Jack of course had been England's centre half for the World Cup win over West Germany in 1966, and then famously become an Irish legend, taking his team to two World Cup final stages. The England game was marred by bad crowd scenes in 1995, but by then Jack became an honorary Irishman. Before the friendly in 2015 Jack was introduced to the 40,000 or so spectators, and got an emotional welcome from both sets of fans.

My thoughts went back to October 1993. Spain were due to visit Dublin for a World Cup qualifier against Jack's Irish team, and he asked me if I would be his guest for the game. I arrived at the Airport Hotel and joined up with the team. Jack and I had a couple of beers and the next morning, I went and joined him for breakfast. Jack told me to have some Shredded Wheat, which at the time he was advertising on TV. I did as I was told but noticed he was having cornflakes. 'Why aren't you having Shredded Wheat?' I asked him. 'Can't stand the stuff,' was his reply! I think he was kidding!

Our trip into Lansdowne Road was cheered by thousands, and as we arrived at the ground Jack took another pal, Des McVey, and me into the pre-match VIP room to do some introductions before he went off to join the team. First, we were met by Ireland Prime Minister Bertie Ahern. Jack said, 'Hello Prime Minister, meet my friends Mike and Des.' Then he took us to Mary Robinson, then the Ireland President, then to singer Chris de Burgh. We got a drink and Ian St John came over to me, 'How do you know all of them? Paddy Crerand isn't happy – he didn't get introduced to that lot!'

Ireland lost to Spain but Jack was held in such regard, that I did not hear a cross word. Later on, I spent the evening with Jack and his wife Pat in their hotel room, watching England get knocked out of the World Cup qualifiers, that made us really pissed off!

I first met Jackie Charlton in 1987, when he already had a fearsome reputation amongst event organisers for tough talking. So, it was with some trepidation that I phoned him to ask if he would speak at my MBN lunch at the Dragonara Hotel in Leeds. He had recently been appointed as the Republic of Ireland manager and was preparing for a European Championship qualifier against Bulgaria. This was an important event for me and I wondered how the fee negotiation would go. I need not have worried – he was the easiest person to deal with. What would be his expenses, I asked, 'I'm coming to Leeds anyway as my wife is looking at wedding dresses for our daughter, so I don't want expenses.' We worked together for twenty years. The fees went up but he was worth every penny.

At the Leeds lunch, he was collared by an Irish guest of the top table sponsors, who did not seem very impressed that Jack was the new Ireland manager, and even less that he was English. However, Jack won him over. The guest wanted to know what team Jack was going to pick for the qualifier. Jack got out a cigarette packet, opened it up, and picked the team. Packie Bonner in goal, Morris at number 2, Steve Staunton at 3, etc. He then signed the packet and gave it to the guest, who by now thought Jack was great! Weeks later the guest phoned me to say the team picked at the lunch was the exact one that played. The fag packet was framed and on his office wall but he did not tell me if he had a bet on the team selection!

Jack went on to love his years in Ireland, but the start was weird to say the least. It began with a call from Des Casey, President of the Irish Football Association, asking would he be interested in doing the job. 'Yes, I would Mr Casey,' was Jack's reply and the line went dead. Many names were bandied around in the next weeks, no one mentioned Jack's, but another call came from Mr Casey to see if he was still interested. 'Yes,' said Jack and the line went dead again. Shortly afterwards Jack got a call from Jimmy Armfield, an ex-England colleague then working for the *Daily Express*, to tell him that he had got the job!

'So, I went to Dublin to discuss terms and money, as you would. I met Mr Casey and the Irish officials. He asked me how much would you be wanting to do the job? Well Mr Casey I'm quite a wealthy lad so how much did you pay Eoin Hand the previous manager?' 'Will you take what we paid him?' they asked me. 'I'll want a lot more than that!' *And he got more!*

Ireland reached the Italia 90 World Cup and Jack Charlton became an Ireland legend by taking them to the quarter finals for the only time. He recalled his team talk before the match against Italy in Rome, "Now I'm due to go fishing back in Ireland in a couple of days, so don't think of winning this bloody game." Like good boys they lost, and we flew in to Dublin to a welcome home with over a million in the streets. After the reception, I caught the first flight the next morning to Newcastle. My pal Denis Woodhead picked me up at the airport and drove me home to see the wife. I picked up my fishing gear, gave the wife a kiss and we drove to Stranraer to catch a ferry to Northern Ireland. We drove across country and re-entered the South at about 6 o'clock. Had a look at the water to check for fish, then saw a pub and went for a pint of Guinness. As we reached the door a big Irishman staggered out and on seeing me he said, 'Arh Jack, it's good of ye to come to me retirement party." I thought Italy to Newcastle to Stranraer to Northern Ireland to the Republic, and this fella thought I was coming to see him.' He did not disappoint the man!

Jack said his trainer in the World Cup was a devout Catholic, and while they were in Rome he asked Jack if he could get the boys in to meet the Pope. Jack said he would try and to his amazement an audience was granted at the Vatican. He thought they would be on their own but there were hundreds on the day. Ireland were the only football team to get the honour but there was a catch, as they had to sit through a blessing ceremony which was fine, but the blessing was not only in English but many languages, and it took a long time. Jack said he was seated quite close to his Holiness, and at the end of each blessing, the Pope would make the sign of the cross to the gathering. 'I must have just dozed off for a moment and as I looked up the Pope was looking straight at me and giving his blessing, not quite realising that he wasn't doing the blessing just to me, I waved back ...'

Jack was honoured with Irish citizenship and bought a house in Ballina, on the west coast – Mary Robinson, the Irish President, comes from there. Local firms carpeted Jack's house for him, while others fitted out the kitchen and laid out the garden as well. Jack loved it and the pay-back was to open the town's salmon festival held each year. In the main street, they had a number of events and races and the organisers asked Jack if he would enter a goose race. The Irish love a gamble and the betting was fierce, Jack went to the start and was given a goose. 'So, you know which is yours we've chalked a number 5 on it.' 'I pointed it up the course, gave it a kick up the arse and it romped home – the organisers were very upset. "Everyone backed your goose and we lost a fortune!" Before the event ended they were back, "Could you start the last race?" So, I went down to the start and it was a blind man's race, six men and their dogs, and one woman were lined up. "Now Jack, here's a flag. Drop the flag and they'll go!" "But they're blind." "Ah yes – drop the flag and shout 'GO'!"

Jack played his football for Leeds United as a tough centre half. He thought an international career had passed him by, until the call came from Alf Ramsey to join the England squad in the run-up to the World Cup Finals, to be held in England in 1966. His first representative honour came in 1965 when he was picked to play for the Football League against the Scottish League at Hampden Park. He made his own way to Glasgow by train. As he arrived at Hampden the first person he met was Alf, later of course Sir Alf, who shook hands. 'He said "Jack Charlton" – that was all he said and didn't speak to me again for a year!' Jack went into the away dressing room, and put his bag by the number 5 shirt. Sitting next to him was, 'A little Japanese fella, in just a jock strap and bottle-top glasses.' 'Nobby Stiles?' asked Jack – 'Yes – Jack Charlton?' was his reply. It was the start of a life-long friendship. Jack went on that Nobby wore contact lenses, not the little plastic jobs you get today, but what looked like whole eyes. He had a bottle of lubricant, a stick with a rubber end to get the lenses out and as he put them in the lubricant ran down his chest, hence the jock strap! 'When they were in he was totally blind for ten minutes. I took him over to a mirror and said, "Nobby they're playing in blue today, if you hit anything in black with a whistle, apologise!"'

'I could never understand why people were scared of Nobby Stiles.' He was to find out in May 1966 when England went on a pre-World Cup short tour to Europe. England were leading Poland by a goal to nil when Jack said 'Someone gave away a daft free kick on the edge of our penalty box.' He always looked sheepish when he told this story, as this time as it was him! 'Nobby had the job of organising the defensive wall. He got Alan Ball and Roger Hunt lined up but next was our kid. Now Bobby liked to hit balls at people but did not like them hitting balls at him, so Nobby got the other two tight but had to lean over and pull Bobby into his place. The free kick was ready to be taken and Nobby grabbed at Bob again, as he did so the Poles took the kick and it whistled past where Nobby should have been. It grazed the post and went for a goal kick. "You silly little prat," I shouted at Nobby, "that nearly cost us." He glared and started to walk towards me – now it's a fact that Nobby Stiles walked faster than he ran. As he got ten yards away, my nerve broke. "Piss off Nobby," I said as I ran away.'

Much was made in the sixties and seventies about vendettas between footballers and many people said that Jack Charlton had a 'little black book' with the names of 'enemies' who were due for retribution when he got a chance. He told me that was not the case. It was a good story, but not true …

However, he recalled a particular match at the Dell, Southampton's old ground. Terry Paine was a right-winger who had played for England with Jack, they were friends and had even roomed together on international duty. On this particular Saturday Jack went into a tackle with Paine. 'Terry committed a foul on me that is still taboo in the game today. He went "over the ball" where one player, me, goes for the ball, and the other player, Paine, goes over the ball and into my shin. I was on the ground and thought "He's broken my leg." The tackle went through my shin pad and the studs caused a major gash that went right down to the bone. 'I got up and hobbled after Paine. When I caught up with him I hit him on the back of the head. He went down and I got on top of him. I got my arm around his neck and was going to strangle him, when an arm went around my neck. It was the referee, Jim Finney. He stood me up and jabbed a finger in my chest, "You big sod, I should send you off for that, but that little bastard got just what he deserved." Jack said, 'Now that is what I call an understanding referee ... Just imagine a Premiership player doing that live on Sky today; they would probably get ten years in Strangeways.'

A footnote to that tale was that years later Jack drove from Newcastle to Hereford to be a surprise guest at Jim Finney's seventieth birthday party. Friends for life. But he does not recall going to any similar parties for Terry Paine!

Usually Jack didn't tell jokes. He did once say that he would occasionally tell a gag that Bernard Manning gave him. 'Use it, Jack. It's clean, so I won't need it again.' He did, however, like to get away from football tales occasionally. One was about a pal who had been in the SAS and was doing protection work. He got a call from a management company who wanted someone to look after an American group on their UK tour. They were the heavily bearded heavy rock band ZZ Top. He attended an interview in the Piccadilly Hotel in Manchester and the band asked him if he had been in the armed forces? 'Aye, the SAS,' he told them. Did he see active service? 'Aye, Falklands and the Gulf.' 'Did you kill anyone?' 'Aye, lots.' 'Did you shoot them?' 'No, I was the cook ...'

Jack and England had a great World Cup but he used to tell us that he never watched film of the game for many years after 1966. Eventually his son Peter brought a copy home from Europe and they sat and watched the whole game in colour. 'When I played it was in black and white.' He went on to talk about the great England captain Bobby Moore 'The game was almost over, the bench were waving their arms to say "Blow the whistle ref" as the Germans broke down the right wing. They knocked a cross into the box and I let go of Uwe Seeler, who I had hold of, but the ball was hit in near the post. "Hell I'm out of position," I thought,

I needn't have worried as Bobby read the move, trapped the ball and as I was yelling at him to kick it into the stands, did he? Did he hell! He passed it to Alan Ball on the edge of the box, got it back and ran into midfield – did he hoof it out? No way! He looked up and hit a fifty-yard pass over Geoff Hurst's shoulder. Geoff nodded it on and blasted the fourth goal into the net, just as Kenneth Wolstenholme was saying the famous lines, "There are people on the pitch. They think it's all over. It is now." I was just looking at the captain and thinking I'll never be able to play this f****** game.'

Jack went on to play in the 1970 World Cup in Mexico, where the Germans got their revenge, beating England 3–2 in the quarter finals. On the plane home Jack saw Sir Alf sitting on his own, and went and sat next to him. 'I said, "I'm almost thirty-five and I've decided that it's probably time for me to retire from international football." He looked at me and all he said was "I totally agree, Jack."'

When Jack was manager of Sheffield Wednesday a few years later he invited me over for an evening game, where he introduced me to his loyal number two, Maurice Setters, a fine player in his own right but with the bandiest legs ever seen on a football pitch. Jack told me that Maurice held a world record; he was the only player ever to have been nutmegged from fifty yards!

Some will remember that Jack had a couple of scary incidents when manager of the Republic of Ireland that resulted in a brain scan. Nothing untoward was found but he did tell me that he was fishing with friends in Ireland and over a few beers the talk got on to football (now there's a surprise). They were discussing a former player at Fulham, and Jack could not remember his name. Jack went to bed but woke up in a sweat, still trying to remember the Fulham player. He got up and was pacing around the kitchen with a cup of tea, and getting more and more agitated. He decided he couldn't put up with this any more so he rang Kenny Dalglish – at two o'clock in the morning. 'Kenny, it's

Jack.' 'Do you know what the time is?' an understandably grumpy Kenny said. 'Yes, but I need to know the name of that fair-haired winger at Fulham in the late sixties.' 'Terry Parmenter. Now bugger off …'

So, it was particularly pleasing to see Jack and Pat at the Ireland versus England game on 8 June 2015 and to see that Charlton smile, eighty years young.

Chapter 8

Wilf McGuinness

Left to Right – Alan Ball, Mike Newlin and Wilf McGuinness.

'I joined Manchester United in 1953, after captaining Manchester, Lancashire and England Schoolboys. I captained the legend that was Sir Bobby Charlton, and even then, I knew that I should not have borrowed his hair brush ...' For those of you who don't remember Wilf McGuinness, he lost his job as the first manager to replace Sir Matt Busby, and that almost certainly contributed to the fact that he was and is as bald as a coot!

'It was February 1969 when Sir Matt called me into his office. "Wilf son, I'm going to retire and you are going to be the new manager of Manchester United." What an honour, and although we got to four major semi-finals in an eighteen-month spell ... we didn't bloody win one of them. So, Sir Matt called me into his office again, "Wilf I don't know what we're going to do without you ... but we're going to try!"'

Wilf's playing career was ended very early by injury at the start of the 1960s so his thoughts turned to coaching. Sir Alf Ramsey and the Football Association got him to coach the England Youth team for a Little World Cup tournament in England in 1963 – his side won the final at Wembley. But it could have been very different. 'We stayed at Butlin's holiday camp in Bognor Regis, along with some of the competing nations. I wanted the boys to bond, so I took them to a local pub. Our party included the likes of John Sissons of West Ham, Ron Harris of Chelsea and Tommy Smith of Liverpool and by closing time they had "bonded" very well. As we got back to our chalets they may have been a little noisy. What I had forgotten was that on the floor above us were the Greek team, and their very irate manager was shouting at us that he was going to report us to the authorities. Being cute, I dashed into a chalet, took off my coat and got ready to pretend that I had been in all evening, when I got sight of the seventeen-year-old Tommy Smith rolling up his sleeves. "You're right Wilf, let's 'do' the Greek bastard," said Tommy. I smoothed that one out but it taught me quite a lesson.'

Wilf had the loudest voice of any speaker that I ever worked with. Quite often he didn't need a microphone. After United he worked in Aris Salonika, Greece, York City, Jordan and had many years at Bury where he ended up as physio and cat feeder. 'If the cat had lived I'd have had a job for life.' Never the shrinking violet, he could fall out with a brick wall, but just as quickly have a joke and pint with his enemies. He recalled a match with Bury reserves at Oldham where he fell out with the opposition's manager. They exchanged insults on the touchline until Wilf, who had won two international caps for England, shouted at the manager, 'Show us your caps.' Getting no response, he was just about to have another pop when one of the subs said, 'Wilf – he's won twenty-eight caps for Northern Ireland.' 'It was one of the only times that I was speechless.'

When he was physio at Bury, he was having knee and hip trouble, so when a player got injured it took Wilf ages to get to him by which time he had usually recovered. On one occasion as he made his way slowly back to the dugout, a Bury fan shouted at him, 'McGuinness, you're living proof that Snow White and Dopey did have a love child!'

After his return to the UK in the mid-1970s Wilf got the opportunity to manage York City. 'I managed York in the 4th Division, 3rd Division and 2nd Division in consecutive seasons, unfortunately in reverse order … You can laugh, but they didn't laugh at York City. When our chairman was asked about my management he thought for a moment … "If McGuinness fell in the River Ouse, it would be a misfortune. However, if someone pulled him out it would be a bloody catastrophe."' So Wilf left Bootham Crescent and, as he put it, he was 'fired with enthusiasm'.

It's well known on the speaking circuit that everybody pinches each other's gags. If one of our hard-working comics comes up with a 'new' story at a sportsman's dinner, you can bet the next night it will be repeated, even hundreds of miles away. Arguments are many, and sometimes very heated, but as the late great Frank Carson would often say, 'It's the way you tell 'em.' Now Wilf was in the dressing room at Bury when the manager, Jim Iley, was asking his right back to 'put their star man out of the game'. His reply was a classic. 'Just for tonight boss or for life?' Wilf thought that was a great line and that he would use it in his next speech. However, he felt that some listeners wouldn't know the Bury player so the story changed as follows. England were playing Portugal in the World Cup semi-final at Wembley in 1966, and Alf Ramsey was giving his team talk. 'Now Portugal are a very good team, but they only have one star player, Eusebio. So, Nobby Stiles, I want you to put Eusebio out of the game. "Just for tonight Alf, or for f****** life?" "No, no, no, Nobby. Just do what's necessary."' Well for Nobby that was a licence to kill. As time went by, I was doing a lunch with Peter

Osgood and Ossie told the 'Nobby and Eusebio' tale, but he swore that it was Bobby Moore who told him about it. Now you know the true story, but to my absolute amazement when Nobby joined the speaker circuit, with the help of Wilf, he started to tell the story himself! So, who writes the jokes? Who cares, as long as they are good and told well, as Frank Carson rightly said …

After leaving Bury FC Wilf renewed the love of his life (other than wife Beryl), and returned to Old Trafford where he still is today, looking after the corporate guests on match days and, yes, making them laugh. 'They still come up to me when I go to Old Trafford and ask for my autograph, but they always look disappointed when they find out that I'm not Duncan Goodhew … or Jap Staam's dad …'

Wilf phoned me after United played at Southampton a few years back. They were wearing their new away strip of grey shirts and had been soundly walloped in the first half. At half time during one of Sir Alex's dressing-downs, the players said, 'It's not our fault boss, we can't see each other in these grey shirts.' In the second half, they changed into white shirts – they still lost, but never wore grey shirts again. Wilf said that he had just come back from doing a speech in Liverpool, and he had been walking to Lime Street Station when he ran into the unlikely sight of a group of local lads wearing the United grey shirts. 'Hello lads, are you *really* United supporters?' 'Piss off, we're burglars, no one can see us in these …'

Wilf had a great career in football, and as a speaker. He was a popular broadcaster on Manchester's Piccadilly Radio but his thoughts were always for Manchester United. He summed up his short spell as manager with the following lines, 'I managed United for four seasons, spring, summer, autumn and winter … the summer was my most successful!'

When I asked Wilf what was the worst defeat he was involved in during his long career, he thought for a moment. 'West Ham versus Bury in the League Cup at Upton Park. Bury lost 10–0, but it was a very even game, they scored five in the first half and five in the second.' Jim Iley, the manager, got the sack. Wilf said it was not just the result. Iley made his centre half, John Bramhall, in charge of calling the offside trap. 'But John had a terrible stammer and by the time he shouted "gggget out", we were two down!'

As I write this, Slaven Bilic is manager at West Ham, having played for the club in the 1990s. Wilf recalled a story told to him by a 'Hammer' from those days. West Ham signed a number of defenders from ex-Yugoslavian countries, when war caused a break up in the region. 'The West Ham keeper came out for a cross, shouted "MINE", and it took twenty minutes to get the Croats and Serbs back on their feet.'

Wilf was just seventeen when he made his debut for Manchester United. Duncan Edwards was injured before the visit of Wolves and Wilf was selected. In the dressing room before kick-off, Wilf's mentor, Sir Matt's number two Jimmy Murphy, saw that Wilf was very nervous. 'Wilf, son, how have you got into this team?' 'By listening to you, Jimmy,' was Wilf's reply. 'Well listen to me now. These Wolves players are here to take your winning bonus, and if they do you won't be able to go home and treat your mother and father. And the player you are marking is an animal, he's called Peter Broadbent.' Wilf said he was now foaming at the mouth. 'Give me the ball, I'll go out and get him.' (Wilf later discovered that Jimmy had been winding him up and that Broadbent was a gentleman footballer.) As they were warming up Peter, who knew it was Wilf's debut, came over and patted Wilf on the back and said, 'Good luck son.' Wilf replied to him with, 'Piss off you thieving bastard!'

Wilf went on to win two caps for England but a horrendous injury virtually finished his playing career. Years later at many events, after much red wine, he would roll up his trouser leg and show off his 'war wound' – whether you wanted him to or not!

Chapter 9

Johnners

Brian Johnston. The cake was commissioned by MBN for Johnner's 80th birthday.

Brian Johnston had one of the most memorable voices that ever graced my events. Commentaries on the Boat Race were followed by many years on BBC television covering cricket Test Matches. He loved radio too, and his *Down your Way* programme made him a household name. It did not matter if you were 'prince or pauper' Brian treated everyone alike and that endeared him to millions. His many years on *Test Match Special* on radio are arguably the performances for which he was most loved. He was already a fixture on the speaking circuit when I came into contact with him personally. Freddie Trueman gave me his number and we soon agreed a lunch in Leeds. It was early in my MBN days and he came to Leeds by train. As was always the case he looked immaculate and those brown and white brogue shoes he wore to every event stand out in my memory.

For an elderly gentleman, Johnners was childlike in his enthusiasm. As I was to find out he loved to tell jokes, often very bad ones, but his infectious laughter soon won over the audience (whoever they were). 'Hello, everyone. Did you hear about …' was how they would start.

'What do you call a Frenchman, blown out of a cannon? Napoleon Blownapart.'

He blamed the next one on F. S. Trueman. 'Did you hear about the "flasher" who was going to retire?' No, Brian would answer. 'Well he has decided to stick it out for another year!'

I am sure you get the drift, so I will resist any more for the moment. He loved his cricket and had a phenomenal memory of players past and present often with full initials – P. B. H. May, M. C. Cowdrey and so on. In the *TMS* box his co-commentators of course often tried to trip him up and make him laugh. Many will recall the most famous incident of all, when Jonathan Agnew, 'Aggers' to Brian, got him with the report that I. T. Botham had tried to hurdle the stumps, but could not quite get his leg over. Johnners almost broke down, as he tried to finish his summing up, egged on by Aggers. Brian had to say, 'Oh do stop it, Aggers.' Drivers all over the country had to pull over as they were laughing so much. After the broadcast Brian was not that impressed that he had been 'got', but at future lunches he gave me an audio tape of the clip and we used it to finish the shows, always to standing ovations. Clever old broadcaster.

Everyone in the *TMS* box had a nickname from Johnners. His old pal Don Mosey was the 'Alderman', Fred was 'Sir Frederick', Trevor Bailey was the 'Boil' and scorer Bill Frindall was the 'bearded wonder'. Geoff Boycott was 'Boycers'. I would love to have been 'Newlers' or 'Miker', but I remained just Mike for all the time I knew him, but I did use to get postcards, often to MBN. Just like the great Ronnie Barker, he loved the saucy seaside cards. I still have them.

On the subject of wind-ups, or slips of the tongue, the *TMS* team got him going during a Test Match against Pakistan, who had a fast bowler called Asif Mahsood. Johnners was reported to have said, live on air, 'Now coming in from the Pavilion end is Massive Arseood.'

He also cackled mischievously during a Test with the West Indies when he got the opportunity to say, 'Welcome back after the tea interval, where the batsman's Holding, the bowlers Willey.' He did also admit that he once told listeners that Ray Illingworth was relieving himself at the Nursery End.

It was Brian who started the tradition of suggesting that the listeners could send in cakes to the box. Hundreds arrived over the years and many (often chocolate cakes) were enjoyed during the Tests. There were so many cakes that children's hospitals, and other worthy causes were grateful recipients of those that were not gobbled up by the team. David 'Bumble' Lloyd told me that he often tried to get Johnners going, and finally succeeded on one memorable occasion. A cake arrived in the box and they gave it to Johnners with a card that Bumble asked him to read out as it was from a lovely old lady. 'Well I have a chocolate cake here from a Tilda Rice, thank you Tilda Rice for our cake. We shall enjoy it.' Comments from the box like 'Is it a rice cake?' fell on deaf ears, until he realised that he had been 'had'.

Brian's career as a cricket player was undistinguished, wicket-keeper for his school 2nd XI was the height of his achievement. However, he became a very welcome player for the Lords Taverners' charity team, playing with such illustrious names as the Duke of Edinburgh, and many of cricket's great names. His most memorable moment was making a stumping off the bowling of the great Australian captain and leg-spinner Richie Benaud, only spoilt by the square leg umpire saying, 'Well done Brian, and it was very sporting to give the batsman so long to get back.'

My saddest day at one of my MBN lunches was as we approached Christmas 1993. I was in the Marriot Hotel in Bristol waiting for Brian to arrive on the train from London. At about 10 o'clock there was a phone call for me. It was Pauline – Brian's wife – to tell me that the wonderful man had had a heart attack in the taxi taking him to the station. It was serious. I said I would ring her later in the day. They say in show business that the show must go on, and it did, but it was very hard to do; telling over 450 guests that Brian was ill was one of the hardest things I have done. I got the commentator Peter Brackley out of bed in Weston-Super-Mare and told him the news and 'Brackers' sped down to Bristol, and spoke brilliantly as usual. Jonners had nearly died, the cabbie doing a great job to get him to hospital, but the attack affected his brain, and the Johnners we loved was gone. The shell that was left fought on and was able to go home, but early in the New Year he passed away. My only solace was Pauline phoning a couple of weeks before he died, to tell me that Brian had got up the night before, got fully dressed at about midnight, including the famous brogues, and when Pauline asked what he was doing he told her that he was going to Mike Newlin's lunch in Bristol …

A few months before the heart attack we had a conversation about whether he would like to do a theatre show with me, based on 'From the Commentary Box'. He was still doing some one-man theatre nights, but he said he was over eighty and felt that he should be slowing down a little. I wonder if he had portents of the future?

'From the Commentary Box' went on to great success in theatres around the UK in Brian's memory. Fred took over the Jonners role, Bumble was his co-commentator, and Graham Gooch was the guest in the box. Of course, we finished every night with the Aggers tape, with his last words on that tape, 'I've stopped laughing now.'

Chapter 10

Tommy Smith

Left to Right – This is one of our 'Hardmen of Soccer' Lunches. Norman Whiteside (who was standing in for Nobby Stiles), my daughter Lisa (who worked for MBN), Tommy Smith and Norman 'Bites yer legs' Hunter.

Liverpool is famous for producing characters, but to call Tommy a character rather states the obvious. He made friends and enemies in numbers, but I never saw him take a backward step and he is proud to be a 'Scouser'.

His love of Liverpool Football Club was forged at an early age, and really took hold when that great manager Bill Shankly took over the reins at Anfield in the late fifties. Tommy was only fifteen when he was taken onto the groundstaff. Tom's dad had died at an early age and his mum struggled with bringing up Tommy, just buying football boots was hard. Shanks took the young apprentice under his wing and would send extra cash home to help out. Shanks hated the summer, no football made him unhappy, so he was always at Anfield, even out of season. The groundstaff had to work all year round, doing jobs like painting and weeding the terraces. One Thursday Shanks told the apprentices to assemble in the car park behind Anfield for a 'match'. As they awaited their opponents to arrive, a couple of bin lorries pulled up and out got eleven dustbin men. They would play until the apprentices won the match. Shanks really did hate the summer.

To say that Tommy would have killed for Shankly was matched by Bill, who said of a young Smith that Tom had not been born, but quarried. He got the nickname 'tank' and the 'Kop' called him the Anfield Iron, and it stuck. He terrorised opponents over a long career, but during one game at Anfield he was threatening murder at the Kop end when a pork chop landed near him, and a voice came from the crowd, 'Have that for your dinner.' Everyone laughed, and that probably saved the opponent's life! Years later Tommy was speaking at a do in Liverpool when someone asked him if he remembered the 'pork chop' incident. He certainly did. 'Well he's sitting over there ...' Tommy went over and the supporter told him that back then he had been a butcher in town, and was taking some meat home. 'I thought the other guy was in danger, so I threw on the chop, in case it was because you were hungry!'

In 1968 Alec Lindsay joined Liverpool from Bury and Tommy and Alec quickly became great mates, not least that they both liked a bet and often discussed the horses as much as football. It was traditional back in the late sixties that on Fridays the whole squad would get together back at Anfield after training, and the players would have a walk on the pitch to get into the right frame of mind for Saturday. Tommy said that Bill Shankly would always call you by your first name if you were in his good books. However, if he used your full name, watch out. On this particular Friday, soon after Alec joined the club, he and Tommy were sitting discussing the afternoon racing at Haydock Park when Tommy saw 'Shanks' making a bee-line for them. 'Have you done anything wrong Alec?' 'No Smithy, nothing.' 'So why is the boss heading this way?' 'No idea.' As the manager arrived he said, 'Hello, Tommy son, are you ready for tomorrow?' 'Raring to go Boss.' 'Good lad. Now Alec Lindsay, how are you?' 'I'm great boss.' 'Aye you might be, Alec Lindsay, but we're not. You played up front in the reserves and didn't get a kick, before that you were in midfield and had a few good touches, but not great.' 'Well I'm doing the best I can.' 'Well that might not be good enough for Liverpool Football Club, Alec Lindsay. When we signed you from Bury what position did you play?' 'I played left back.' 'No you didn't.' 'I certainly did, I was there!' 'So, Alec Lindsay, who was that fair-haired player in midfield?' 'That was Jimmy Kerr.' 'No it wasn't.' 'Yes it was.' Shanks turned to find his first lieutenant, 'Bob Paisley, we signed the wrong f****** player ...' Alec was moved to left back and went on to become an Anfield favourite and played left back for England.

Tommy's best pal was another England full back, Chris Lawler. He was a man of very few words. In those days players shared hotel rooms for away trips, and Tommy would share with Chris. Even then he got few words out of Chris. 'I'd get up first and ask Chris did he want tea or coffee?' 'Tea.' 'What do you want for breakfast?' 'Toast.' 'What about a paper?' '*Mirror.*' – this went on for years. It came to a head during a Merseyside derby match, never a game that Liverpool liked to lose. Tommy got caught in possession by Everton's winger Johnny Morrissey, who crossed for Joe Royle to score. Tommy shouted at Chris, 'How many words is "Man on!"?' No comment from Lawler. Later in the first half, Tommy slipped again, blamed Lawler, and Liverpool were two down. Tommy had just been made captain and Bill Shankly was not going to be pleased, understatement! 2–0 down but luckily things changed in the second half. New boy Steve Heighway on Liverpool's left wing had a purple patch, and they got back to 2–2. Not long before full time, Heighway got away on the left, his cross was met by John Toshack and his header landed on the six-yard line from where Chris Lawler cracked in the winner. Tommy ran up to congratulate the match winner. 'Smithy, I never called for that one either ...'

Five-a-sides at the training ground were feisty affairs, and played at the end of the training session. Shanks played in the matches and arguments were regular occurrences. One day, Chris Lawler was out injured and watching from the sidelines. Shanks had a shot that beat the keeper but went over the small goals. 'Goal!' shouted the boss but 'Over the top' said Ronnie Yeats. 'Never! It was well in,' said Shanks. Well the argument almost came to blows, which was not unusual, until Shanks saw Chris hobbling along. 'Chris, was it a goal?' 'Over,' was the one-word answer. 'You never speak, Chris Lawler. And when you do you f****** LIE!'

When he left Liverpool, Shanks's industrial language saw him have one of the shortest broadcasting careers, with Radio Merseyside. They sent him to Nottingham Forest for a cup tie with Liverpool. Forest took the lead through a young striker called Gary Birtles, when the lead commentator said, 'Well, Bill, have you ever heard of Gary Birtles before tonight?' 'Well I've f****** heard of him now.' That marked the end of Bill's time on Radio Merseyside.

Tommy worried about Bill when he left the club. He would go and watch games around the North, but his favourite was

Deepdale to watch Preston North End. Bill loved Sir Tom Finney, and they would meet up at games. Once Bill had watched Preston play Sheffield United and the star on the night was a fine midfield man for Sheffield, later to play for England, Tony Currie. In the players' lounge after the game a young reporter on the *Lancashire Post* saw his opportunity to speak to 'Shanks'. 'Mr Shankly, what did you think about the performance of Tony Currie?' 'Aye son, he was very good.' The lad pushed his luck, 'How would you compare him to the great Tom Finney?' 'Aye son, I would think they were equal.' The reporter was amazed, 'You think Currie was equal to Tom Finney?' he asked, looking for clarification. Shanks replied 'Well, you have to remember that Tom is over sixty-five!'

Tommy finished his career with Liverpool, and spent some time playing in the USA – he loves the States and had a holiday home there for many years. When he came home his ex-Liverpool colleague John Toshack had become manager of Swansea City, who were at the time in Division 3. John contacted Tom and Ian Callaghan, the former England winger, to help out, at the Welsh club. They were allowed to travel down for matches, but it worked well, and promotion to Division 2 followed. Tommy would also help with coaching as Toshack still played some games. It was well known that Tommy did have a short fuse on occasion and Tosh got the full force of it once. During one game Toshack, who was on the bench, called out to Smithy that he wanted to come on, and Tommy was to be substituted. This did not go down very well (to say the least). 'I had travelled down with "Cally" and I wanted to play, not have to sit on the bench, but Tosh said "I'm the manager, and I say who will be sub, so get on the bench." There may have been a few harsh words!' A couple of games later Tommy was nursing an injury, so Tosh asked him to look after the bench and subs, so as he said 'I was manager for the day', and John was playing up front. About thirty minutes into the match Tommy told a young substitute to warm up, then to get ready to go on. The lad got ready and Tommy told the linesman that he wanted to make a substitution. Tommy jumped out of the box and waved at John Toshack – Tosh looked around to see who was injured but Tommy called, 'Off you come, Tosh. Get your arse on the bench.' Despite his protests, Tommy told him that *he* was in charge for the match. Tommy was not subbed again.

Chapter 11

Bumble 29 June 2015

Left to Right – Graham Lloyd, Mike Newlin and Graham's Dad "Bumble".

David Lloyd is featured in the newspapers today, as he has been involved in senior cricket for fifty years. He was eighteen when he signed professional at Old Trafford for Lancashire and has played for the county and England with distinction. He went on to become a first-class umpire, before famously turning to coach the England Test side, then a further change of direction as he joined the Sky commentary team, where his humour and knowledge make him the best in the business. I've known him since his testimonial year for Lancs, and, oh I forgot, he was an author, with a book on the challenges of playing against the Aussies – Denis Lillee and Jeff Thomson in particular, who regularly tried to kill 'Bumble' in the 1974-5 tour. He called his book *Gooday you Pommie Bastard*. Seeing him hit in the protector and lying poleaxed on the ground is one of the most painful-looking things I've ever seen on a cricket ground, and I was only watching on telly!

We did a superb theatre tour in 1994. 'From the Commentary Box' was a tribute to Jonners, who had passed away before we could take the show on the road, but David took over the lead role. As the shows started in February it was not a surprise that 'Bumble' walked on stage with a brolly up to welcome the guests, 'Well it's raining here in Buxton, so we're going to have a chat.' In fact, on that night we were in the famous Buxton Theatre, it had snowed heavily, and we all thought the place would be empty, but they are a hardy lot in Derbyshire. The local farmers must have got the tractors out and we were able to start on time at 8 o'clock, with a full house of 800 in the audience.

It reminded 'Bumble' of the famous match between Derbyshire and Lancashire on 2 June 1975 when it snowed in Buxton, and cricket was impossible. I could not believe it as I was on the beach in Cornwall, with the family! Lancs had scored well over 400 on day 1. On day two it snowed. The Buxton ground was six inches deep in snow and play was obviously abandoned. Day three (the county games were three days in those days) and the sun was shining. The Derby players turned up expecting to travel to Hampshire for the following county game in Southampton. Umpire Harold 'Dicky' Bird inspected the pitch and went into the dressing room with the news that the match was on. Nobody could believe it but Dicky was adamant. Derby were skittled out in the first innings in no time flat, followed on and were soon knocked over a second time by the Lancashire fast bowlers. They were able to travel south after all, with one of the biggest innings defeats of all time in the record book, and the certainty that Dickie Bird was barmy!

People used to ask David about how he got the 'Bumble' nickname and in those days, he used to blame his dad who was a music fan, and supposedly named him after the lead singer of 'B Bumble and the Stingers'. 'If you think that's bad,' he would add, 'my brother was called "Dave Dee Dozy Beaky Mick and Tich"!'

My favourite tale from the late sixties at Lancashire involved the county's new signing, the Indian Test wicket-keeper Farokh Engineer. In one of his first games in the County Championship they were playing Kent at Old Trafford, 'Bumble' was in his customary fielding position at leg slip and the bowler was England's opening 'quickie' Peter Lever. Batting for Kent was one of the last of the breed of footballing cricketers, Stuart Leary, who played for Charlton Athletic in the winter. Lever bowled a quick one outside off-stump which Leary went after and got a big nick. Farokh was seen to dive and roll over claiming a catch. Leary looked back, tucked his bat under his arm, and walked off. 'Well, I walked over to Frank Hayes and Jack Simmons in the slips, "Did you see that lads, it looked as though it might not have carried?" "Bounced about a yard short," said Jack, so I slowly walked over to Engineer. "Well caught 'Rookie', but the lads had a thought that the ball might just have bounced?"' Farokh looked at him and came out with 'Only once'!

One of David's early memories of joining the *Test Match Special* commentary team involved 'Jonners' of course, and the famous chocolate cakes. Brian cut a large slice of chocolate fudge cake, and just as 'Bumble' had taken a large mouthful Johnners asked him if he would comment on the technicalities of away swing bowling from close to the stumps. There was much mirth from colleagues in the 'box'. 'I did get my own back on occasions, but Brian was the maestro.'

In Australia in 1974 the boys went to an Australian Ladies presentation night and the master of ceremonies introduced them to the guests: 'In the audience tonight we have the England cricket touring side, I hope all you ladies give them the clap they deserve ...'

Bumble was one of the best speakers for me, and on the after-lunch or dinner scene, Lancashire cricket has boasted a number of great speakers over the years. Mike Watkinson and Graeme

Fowler were excellent and later Bumble's son Graham joined the distinguished list. Graham played for Lancs and the England one-day team. When Graham scored his maiden first-class century, a local newspaper announced that, 'Graham Lloyd son of West Indian legend Clive Lloyd made his first 100 for Lancashire.' David also recalled meeting a lady member in the women's pavilion who asked him, 'Are you related to Clive?' 'Yes, we're brothers,' Bumble replied. 'I thought so,' she said.

When the county chairman met Farokh Engineer, early in his stay at Old Trafford, hostilities had commenced between India and Pakistan and as the situation reached crisis point a concerned chairman chatting to Rookie asked him, 'Is there any likelihood of you having to return home to fight?' Farokh's reply was, 'Only if the fighting reaches my village will I go back to protect my wife and children.' 'Where is your village, Farokh?' The reply: 'Altrincham.' Rookie still lives near Altrincham, and is a popular man when he visits Old Trafford. F. S. invited him to his sixty-fifth birthday bash in London and there is a fine picture of him and a bevy of greats signing bats at Fred's 'do' which I have put in this book.

David was never afraid to voice his opinions; they did not always get approval of the English Cricket Board.

On Muttiah Muralithuran's bowling action: 'If that action is legal we should coach it.'

In 1989 he was in trouble again for suggesting that England had 'murdered' Zimbabwe during a drawn Test – that got him in trouble with the whole of Zimbabwe, as well as the ECB.

Against Pakistan there was controversy over the reverse swing that Wasim Akram and Waqar Younis got on the cricket ball, but it was a golf match that got Bumbie's goat. On this occasion, he played with Wasim at a charity golf day at Dunham Forest in Altrincham. They were in the same four-ball and when 'Was' drove off the first, the ball went away like a left hander's cover drive. Wasim wandered off down the adjoining fairway, where he was seen to hack the ball several times. When they finally met up on the first green, David sank a putt for a five on a par four. Wasim had a chip and a couple of putts, 'How many was that Bumble?' 'Five Was.' 'Good, I got a five as well!'

Chapter 12

Snooker and 'that' Final

Left to Right – Steve Davis, Mike Newlin and Denis Taylor. We re-created the World Snooker Championship final of 1985 (Denis won again!)

I always thought that snooker would be good at my lunches, the idea of having a full-size table and an audience of around 200, with banter with the guests and finishing with trick shots was a formula that would work well. My first choice to break off the idea was the former World Snooker Champion Ray Reardon, and it proved a good one. 'Dracula' as he was nicknamed mixed well with the guests at the first event in the (now gone) Elizabeth Suite in London City, but it was not the 'chat' that amazed me but the practice frame. I had found a lovely firm in Birmingham who made and hired out tables. They were just finishing setting up as Ray arrived at 11 a.m. He got out his cue, ordered a tea, and proceeded to make a complete clearance of 137.

He had never seen the table. He was brilliant. To put it in to perspective, as many will know, a maximum snooker break is 147, and even at the World Championships in Sheffield at the Crucible 147s are rare, and the players play and practise hundreds of frames.

My next player was the 1985 World Champion Dennis Taylor. We went over to Belfast to do a lunch at the Europa Hotel, and this time the format included a one-frame match à la Pot Black. His opponent was another former World Champion, Canadian Cliff Thorburn. Dennis called him 'The Snail' for his slow play, but he was a great bloke, Dennis had much banter with his 'home' audience ...

'My Grandad came from up the road, and loved fishing. He went out one very foggy morning in the middle of winter, and it was so cold he had to cut a hole in the ice to get his line in. After a while a voice came from up above, 'There are no fish in there.' Grandad was shocked and called out, 'Is that you God?' The reply came 'No, it's the ice rink manager!'

Dennis is a lovely bloke and a fabulous speaker, and I was always looking for ways to use him at my events, and in 2004 I gave him a call to discuss a new idea for some lunches with a snooker table for 2005.

Now where were you at just after midnight on 29 April 1985?

I was at home in Brooklands on the Manchester–Trafford border watching, with 18.5 million others, the closing frame of the World Snooker Championship in Sheffield between Dennis and World Champion Steve Davis. The score was seventeen frames all, and the whole championship came down to the final frame, and then not just the frame but the last ball. Whoever sank the black ball would lift the trophy. Of course, it has gone down in sporting history that Taylor potted the black, waved his cue to a cheering audience and shook hands with a visibly upset Steve Davis. It made television history, too, with the highest audience for any event on television after midnight, a record that stands to this day.

So back to 2004, and my conversation with Dennis: 'What about us recreating "that" final frame at some lunches next year. Do you think that Steve would be up for it?'

'I very much doubt it, but I'll give him a call,' was Dennis's reaction.

Was he up for it? He certainly was, and so we agreed that a series of MBN lunches would begin in 2005 at the Forte Crest in Birmingham. It was my first meeting with the great six-times World Champion, who he drove up from his home in Brentwood in Essex. Of course, his manager was Barry Hearn, who was based in Romford, where I was born and bred, so we had some common ground, but I spoiled that when I said that I would look after his snooker cue and take it to the banqueting room, while he had a cuppa with Dennis. He gave me a look that froze my bones. NOBODY could look after his cue. Bad start, but later in the 'tour' he did let me look after it, well I was paying him a few bob!

Steve would joke to the audience that everybody in snooker had a nickname, except him. 'Whirlwind' Jimmy White, 'Hurricane' Alex Higgins, 'Big Bill' Werbeniuk and so on. 'I was so boring as I had no nickname, but after some years I became known as "Interesting".'

Any mention of Canadian Bill Werbeniuk got him going on who he hated playing and 'Big Bill' was on the list – fortunately Dennis Taylor wasn't! 'You might not remember that Bill had a nervous problem when he played and used beta blockers to help his problem. To add to the situation he also drank very large amounts of lager to balance things out. He would have a couple of pints before the match, then another pint during every frame, then at the break during the match he would have a couple of pints and after the match would have a pint or two. Just imagine if a nineteen frame match went the whole way, he would consume 20–30 pints of lager!' But Steve went on to say that that was not the worst of it. Drinking so much booze would have a predictable side effect. 'Bill would often break wind, and if he missed a shot he would leave you right in it.' But the worst was still to come when, 'After one shot Bill managed to screw back, and follow through at the same time ...'

For our opener it was decided that I would be the referee. Now I had done a few practice shots and Steve asked what my best break had been – 'Minus seven,' I joked and 'Yes I can see that,' was his response. However, I could not muck up the refereeing could I? Well I can say that I did very well, so there. I borrowed some white cotton gloves from the chef at the Forte Crest and the match got under way. Dennis potted the first red 'One' then a black 'Eight' then a red 'Nine'. 'Boy, he speaks German,' came from Dennis. Well the frame went on and as it came to a close, Dennis needed to pot the black to win the frame, and bring back the memories of twenty years before ... He potted it, gave that famous wave and Steve cried of course. This happened at every venue we went to, wasn't Steve unlucky!

They only played the one frame but the boys would then both do some brilliant 'trick' shots to close the show. Dennis would finish with a shot that involved a lady from the audience (preferably one wearing a short skirt) and I was given the job of selecting the volunteer, or should I say 'sucker'? In Manchester, I had the opportunity to select one of my own accountants, who had a table. The partner chosen was Lesley Haresnape and she willingly agreed. Dennis got her to clamber onto the table, lay flat out and hold a 'chalk' in her mouth. He would then tell a gag, asking her not to laugh as she would swallow the chalk. Laugh she did but after recovering was composed enough to let Dennis put a snooker ball onto the chalk, he would then hit a cue ball from the cushion, knock off the ball in Lesley's mouth and pot it in the corner pocket. Easy, I hear you say, well just try it at home on the wife. Lesley dismounted with dignity intact (she is still my accountant), the boys got a standing ovation and we became great pals.

We were due to take the snooker show to Glasgow. I don't know if a Scots audience struck fear into a London boy like Steve, but he was unavailable, so I rang yet another World Champion, this time the fantastic Stephen Hendry and he was happy to stand in for Davis. Well he'd also won a few world titles. He was great fun and when the show moved on to Edinburgh later in the year, Steve Davis was back in the harness, so Dennis was able to tell a story about Stephen Hendry that he did not dare to tell in Glasgow with Stephen there!

Players were often asked who amongst their colleagues was the most 'careful' with money? Stephen Hendry was top of the list. Dennis recalled that after Stephen won his first world title at the Crucible he invited his family, who had been watching his triumph, out to dinner. He took them to a Little Chef in Sheffield and they all had an all-day breakfast, but a young relative left a couple of sausages, so the ever-thrifty Hendry asked a waiter if he could have a doggy bag to take away the left-overs. To which his young relative told the whole restaurant, 'Yippee, we're getting a dog!' He also said that Stephen once spent several hours on a 'pay as you leave' bus in Glasgow.

Chapter 13

Superstition

I'm not especially superstitious. However, at the lunches we always avoided having a Table 13 – it wasn't worth the risk – so, keeping the tradition going, I'm avoiding a Chapter 13 as well …

Chapter 14

Sandy Jones and the PGA

Left to Right – Sandy Jones, Mike Newlin, Peter Alliss and Dave Thomas (former Captain of the PGA and famous golf course designer)

Following the Scottish Speaker of the Year lunch in 2000, won by Gordon Brown, I got a call from Sandy Jones who had competed along with Dougie Donnelly and Ron Yeats. Sandy was then chief executive of the Professional Golfers' Association. He has recently retired as CEO of the PGS and has become chairman of the Golf Foundation Charity. He wondered if I might be interested in organising a Christmas lunch for the PGA? We agreed that London would be the appropriate place, and a December date was fixed for 2001 at my best venue, the Grosvenor House Hotel in Park Lane. As 2001 was to be a Ryder Cup year at the Belfry Course in Birmingham we agreed that our first guest of honour should be the captain of the Europe Ryder

Cup team, Sam Torrance. Planning was going very well and by September several hundred guests were booked in.

Then, on 11 September, came the greatest tragedy of the attack on the Twin Towers in New York. I was in Manchester with Doreen, when we heard the news on the car radio. The shock was touchable and we went home to watch the horror unfold on the television. My thoughts did not consider the upcoming PGA lunch in December, but as events around '9-11' unfolded it became clear that the Americans were not going to come to the UK for the Ryder Cup that was only weeks away. I spoke to Sandy, who, as one of the main organisers of the Ryder Cup, had much more than our lunch on his mind, but we agreed that our event would definitely go ahead, whatever happened with the Ryder Cup. Within days the match was cancelled and it was agreed that it would be postponed until 2002, still at the Belfry. Sandy Jones had not been a professional golfer, but he was a brilliant administrator, and his team at the PGA worked tirelessly to change the arrangements for the following year. Every organisation pulled together and when GB and Europe won in 2002, Sandy had cemented his place in golfing history.

At the Grosvenor House in December 2001, the roof almost came off as Sam Torrance walked to top table, carrying the Ryder Cup trophy, and Sam was to be interviewed on stage by the BBC commentator Dougie Donnelly. All went well until Sam went for a pee break after the lunch and before the speeches. When he came back Sam looked a little 'nervous' and when it came time for him to go on stage, I began to worry that the red wine might have taken effect. Of course, the subject of '9-11' had to be mentioned and I could sense Dougie getting nervous, which was not like him. He caught my eye and suggested we cut the interview short, I said carry on, but I was worried. Dougie then came to the fateful moment and asked about the people who had caused such horror in New York – the Ryder Cup captain uttered the fateful words 'That we should f*** the terrorists!' This brought gasps and even more cheers, Sandy went white but I brought proceedings to a close. There was a table full of journalists and Sandy went around to see how the comment had been viewed and luckily it was never reported in the press. Our PGA lunch continues to this day, with my daughter Lisa running it under her PT Events banner.

Sandy is a classy and interesting speaker, having a great knowledge of the history of golf and the Ryder Cup in particular. He is approaching twenty-five years as chief executive so has been deeply involved in the rise to dominance of Europe in the Ryder Cup, but it might have been different.

In September 1985, the event was held at the Belfry and Sandy was a relatively new member of the executive. On the Saturday, he was given the opportunity to referee one of the afternoon foursomes matches between José María Cañizares and José Rivero for Europe against the American pair of Tom Kite and Calvin Peete. Sandy stupidly thought it would be a cake walk until they reached a green and both balls were about the same distance from the flag. The players asked Sandy who was to putt first. Sandy looked and said it was the USA to go first and Tom Kite, who until then had been quiet said, 'Are you sure?' Sandy broke out in a cold sweat, no he was not sure, so he paced it out and said the USA to play, 'I want a measure' said Kite, and Sandy realised that he had not got a tape measure with him. Tom Kite was now in a rage, and Sandy could see his career going down the toilet. Happily, it was resolved and the Americans lost heavily. Sandy was wary of treading on toes in the future, but Kite did forgive him ... eventually.

As my friendship with Sandy grew we saw the Christmas events in London were growing each year, with over a thousand guests attending, and we also successfully celebrated the centenary of the PGA in 2001. At each event, we raised many thousands of pounds for charities, including the PGA Benevolent Fund that helps pro golfers who have fallen on hard times. Sandy suggested that the PGA Scotland (where he had started his golfing career), could enjoy a Christmas lunch. We asked one of

Scotland's great golfing characters, Brian Barnes, to be our guest of honour, and amazingly nearly 800 came to the Thistle Hotel in Glasgow. I had also asked Elaine C. Smith to speak at the event. Now I expected Rab C. Nesbitt's wife 'Mary doll' to turn up, but no chance – Elaine is a very elegant woman, and during her speech she gently chided the male-dominated world of Scottish golf, and got a standing ovation. We also raised lots of cash for Scottish golfing good causes, so Scotland became an annual event, and like London, is still going strong.

I was delighted that the PGA asked me to become a business partner and at our annual get-together we would finish with a game of golf, usually on one of our great courses. At my last visit, my team, including snooker supremo Barry Hearn, won the PGA Partners trophy at Celtic Manor. It was the first round to be played on the course planned for the Ryder Cup. My name sits proudly on the trophy. What I can reveal is that my personal contribution to our winning total was two points, in a Stableford score of lots, but look on the cup and it says Mike Newlin – I'll settle for that.

My only sadness in the PGA years was that when I sold MBN I finished hosting the events before our Christmas lunch in 2007, and so I missed out on the visit of the great Seve Ballesteros.

Chapter 15

Nobby Stiles

Left to Right – Norbert Stiles (yes that was his real name!), Mike Newlin and Alan Ball, Nobby's midfield partner in 1966.

When England won the Jules Rimet trophy in 1966, one of the enduring images, still as evocative today, was of a little bloke, socks round his ankles, dancing round the touchline with a massive smile. Norbert Stiles of Manchester United and England was that man. He was small and thin and struck terror into opponents both in England and around the world. It was not until long after he retired as a player, and later coach, that Nobby became an after-lunch or -dinner speaker, albeit a reluctant one in the early days. It was his old pal from United, Wilf McGuinness and a lovely event organiser Murray Birnie, who persuaded Nobby that people would want to hear stories from the Old Trafford 'hard man'.

Nobby's opener was always that it took him over half an hour to get to the ground for his trial for United – he only lived around the corner from Old Trafford, but his dad gave him a lift. His dad was an undertaker, Charlie Stiles, and he took him in the hearse … That story had a whiff of Wilf McGuinness about it but from then on Nobby got the crowd going with his footballing stories.

Why Nobby? Well he hated the name Norbert, but Sir Matt Busby would not call him Norbert or indeed Nobby. In Scotland he would have been called Norrie, and to Sir Matt he was always Norrie throughout Matt's life.

When Nobby got a call from Alf Ramsey, it was to make his debut for England Under 23s. The game was to be against Scotland in Aberdeen. Nobby wore contact lenses, and forgot to take them with him up north. He was in a mad panic as it was well known that his eyesight was terrible, and if Alf had realised that he had been unprofessional in his preparation, he might never be picked to play for the full England team. It was a midweek game and Nobby got through the first half under the Pittodrie floodlights, but at half-time Alf was concerned that Charlie Cooke, the Chelsea star, was causing England problems and it was suggested that Nobby might 'sort Cooke out'. Nobby happily agreed and his chance came early on. The ball landed close to Charlie and Nobby hit him with a 'hard' challenge. 'I was looking for a response, when Norman Hunter came running over.' 'What have you done, Nob?' 'I've clobbered Charlie Cooke.' 'Look again,' said Hunter. It was Billy Bremner! Billy said, 'Stilesy you bastard, I'll get you for that.' 'He chased me for the rest of my career but never got me at Leeds United or for Scotland!'

Selection for the World Cup squad followed and Nobby met up with the man he argued most with, big Jack Charlton, who used to call him that little Japanese fella when he was wearing his bottle-top glasses. He also scared Jack during the pre-world cup tour to Poland, as Jack recalled in his chapter.

Nobby also remembered a chat with Alf about Bobby Charlton during training at Lilleshall. 'Alf called me and Alan Ball over. "Have you got a dog?" he asked. "I have," said Bally. "And do you throw him a stick?" "Yes boss." "And what does he do?" "Well he chases it and fetches it back." "Exactly," said Alf. "Now that's what I want you and Nobby to do for Bobby. You get the ball, and give it to him, and let him go and play ..."'

Nobby caused quite a controversy during the 1966 World Cup game against France, when he hit the Frenchman Jacques Simon with a frightening tackle. The referee took no action, but an FA official in the stand told Alf that Nobby should be dropped. Alf said to Nobby that he told the FA that if Nobby was dropped they would need to find a new manager, as he would leave. When he saw Nobby he asked him if he had meant to injure Simon. 'I told him no, I hadn't meant to hurt him, but had mistimed my tackle,' and that was the end of it. Nobby claimed that Jack Charlton had said, 'What's wrong with kicking a Frenchman?'

In the 1966 quarter-final England played Argentina and won 1–0 by a goal from Geoff Hurst, who had replaced the injured Jimmy Greaves. Nobby hated the way the Argentinian players would spit at opponents, and Sir Alf called them 'animals'. Even after the game the Argentina team wanted to get into the England dressing room for a fight. They were stopped, but big Jack shouted out 'Let the bastards in.' Nobby remembered, 'I was looking through Jack's legs and said, "You're right, Jack, let them in" – but I don't know if I would have been so brave if they had actually let them in though!'

Nobby was a committed Catholic and on the morning of the World Cup final, he was up at the crack of dawn and had gone out before breakfast to find the local Catholic church. They were staying in the Hendon Hall Hotel in North London, and whilst out he met George Cohen who asked where Nobby was going. 'You won't find a church here,' George laughed. 'Why not

George?' 'You're in Golders Green – the most Jewish area in London. Will a synagogue do?'

In May 1968, Manchester United won the trophy that most football people wanted when they beat Benfica 4–2 at Wembley to take the European Cup home. It was the accolade that Sir Matt Busby had missed out on with what happened at Munich in 1958. Now ten years on Nobby, who had been a 'Busby babe' but not then in the first team, was able to share an emotional night for the 'Boss' and Eusebio was not able to weave his magic, thanks in part to the performance of 'Norrie' Stiles.

United qualified to play Estudiantes of Argentina in the World Club Championship. The first leg of the tie was to be in Buenos Aires and the reception United, and Nobby, in particular, got was hostile to say the least. Revenge for 1966 was on the agenda, and United were not disappointed. When they arrived in the airport a large crowd were gathered with placards, Denis Law was 'El Rey' (The King). George Best was 'El Beatle', Nobby was 'El Bandido' (The Bandit). 'Charming, this is going to be hard,' he said. He was right. During the game, it seemed that every decision went against the 'Reds'. Nobby was playing inside right for this game and in the second half a brilliant pass from Paddy Crerand put Nobby through on goal, the linesman did not flag but the referee blew for offside. 'I called over to Bobby Charlton, "There's nowt doing for us tonight, the ref's blind." The referee came running over and asked what I had said so I shouted to Bob that he was f****** deaf as well.' Nobby was sent off.

As Nobby left the dressing room looking for the safety of the team bus, he felt something hard being pushed into his back. 'A voice said, "Steeles, you will die. I will kill you, English bastard, Bandido."' Nobby froze, then, as he looked round, it was Brian Kidd!

Denis Law was called the King in Argentina. He was certainly one of Scotland's greatest strikers. He still lives in Cheshire and is almost an honorary Englishman, I don't think! Nobby got his first full cap against the Jocks at Wembley in 1965 and five United men played – Denis and Paddy Crerand for Scotland and Bobby Charlton, John Connelly and Nobby for England. After training at United the players were to go by train to London, different trains of course! Paddy went up to shake hands with Nobby and the other two, but Denis almost ignored them. Nobby was upset but as they lined up in the Wembley tunnel before the game Nobby still went over to shake hands with the 'Lawman'. Denis greeted him with, 'F**** off, you English bastard.' Nobby went on to mention this incident, 'When Denis speaks he tells this story, and in it he says that it was a bad mistake, because "Stiles kicked me all over Wembley that day" … And I did!'

Nobby never got a testimonial from Manchester United, so in 2006, after I had left MBN Promotions, I decided to do a couple of events for Nobby. The PFA thought it was okay and could qualify as a testimonial. So, I planned to talk to Nobby's son, John, and I met the United secretary, who thought they would help. Unfortunately, my deal with MBN blocked me for three years so I had to drop out and sadly no events took place

Nobby, like all the 1966 players, got £1,000 for winning the World Cup. What do you think this would be worth today?

Chapter 16

Jackie Blanchflower

Left to Right – Jackie Blanchflower, Mike Newlin and Bestie. Jackie survived the Munich Air Disaster in 1958, but became one of the top comedians on the speaking circuit.

The first Saturday in May was always FA Cup Final day when I was a lad. I never moved from the telly from dawn until dusk and it cemented my love of football. In 1957 Manchester United played Aston Villa and it was memorable for a horrific challenge by Peter McParland of Villa on the United keeper, Ray Wood. Wood had to leave the field and, as there were no subs in those days, into goal went the United centre half, Jackie Blanchflower. He did a good job until Ray Wood came back for the last few minutes, but not in goal! He was unable to help United, who lost the game. Then came the Munich disaster and, although he survived the crash, Jackie was badly injured and never played again. Manchester United did not look after him very well, indeed he had to leave his club-owned house in 1959. The club tried to make amends in later years, but Jackie rarely went to watch any games at Old Trafford.

Jack's wife Jean was a top nightclub singer and it was Jean who persuaded Jackie to get up and tell a few gags at a Manchester club. He took to it like a duck to water and was eventually to find a new career as a speaker. This only developed well enough to pay the bills in later life so before then he had to do a variety of accounts-based jobs.

Jackie had a spell working for the Demmy bookmaking organisation. The Demmys are a famous Manchester family. Started by Gus Demmy in the 1930s, the bookmaking business was built by Gus's son Selwyn, who grew the firm into one of the betting giants in shops and on the racecourses. Selwyn's brother Harvey was not a great fan of the betting world, but with his brother owned and ran a famous club in Manchester, frequented by a lot of Manchester footballers, notably George Best and Mike Summerbee. Blinkers was a top place to go in the sixties. Harvey went on to build a successful event organising company and he was a tremendous supporter of my lunches, and was a great help to me, his advice and experience being very valuable.

Jackie did many events for me. He would recall how he arrived in England with his brother, the famous Tottenham Hotspur captain Danny, in the late forties. 'Where we came from in Northern Ireland we had never seen traffic lights, we saw red as danger and green was for the IRA. I said to Danny that they don't give those Orangemen much time.'

He went to Old Trafford as a Busby Babe, and won full international caps for Northern Ireland. His preferred position was centre half and when asked about losing his hair, he would blame the heavy 'T' ball they would play with. 'If you saw that ball coming out of the dark sky on a wet November Saturday, and coming straight on to your head lace down, you will know why, when I see a bald man today, I know that he was a good header of the ball.'

If the players had stomach problems in those early days, the trainer at Old Trafford had a potion for every occasion. Jack had a touch of constipation on one morning, so when he got showered he asked the trainer if he could help? 'Certainly, Jack,' he was told and a foul-looking (and tasting) liquid was produced. 'Now Jack how long does it take you to get home?' 'Will I be walking or running?' Jack asked. 'Oh you'll be running,' was the trainer's dead-pan response.

I can't start to sum up 'shaggy dog' stories that he told but perhaps this one will give you a flavour of the man's look on life.

'After the first Gulf War, Ireland discovered that they had not signed a peace treaty with Saddam Hussein so we were still at war with Iraq. So, the Minister of War 'Paddy' phoned Saddam to tell him that he was still at war with Ireland. 'How many planes have you got Paddy?' 'Well we've got a dozen Aer Lingus passenger planes, and McGonagle has a few crop sprayers, so fifteen in total.' 'We have 500 MiG fighters with bombing capacity.' 'Oh, I'll get back to you tomorrow.' Next day Paddy phoned again, 'The war's still on Sadman.' 'Well how many tanks have you got Paddy?' 'Err, I'll get back to you.' Next day Paddy phoned, 'Hello Sadass, the war is still on.' 'OK Paddy how many troops are ready to fight.' 'Well, with about fifty conscripts we can send about a hundred into battle.' 'We have 1 million, highly trained and armed guards.' 'Right, I'll phone tomorrow.' Next day Paddy phoned, 'Hello, Madman, the war's off.' 'Why is that Paddy?' 'We haven't got room for a million prisoners of war!'

I hope that gives you a picture of the sort of comedian Jackie was, barmy but lovely. He would look at a guest during lunch, after one of his stories, and ask, 'How do you confuse an idiot?' They would often say they did not know. 'There – you're confused arc you nut?'

As he got older ill health dogged Jackie and his heavy drinking took a huge toll on him, but when he was announced to speak at any event the light would come into his eyes and the performer took over. With some of his stories you could see the audience wondering if they were true or just his gag to get a laugh. It came home to me as we travelled together from Manchester by train to London to do an event at the Comedy Club with Stan Matthews as guest of honour. At the evening event, there was quite a noisy crowd in, who listened politely to the great Sir Stan, then laughed at the brilliant Jackie Blanchflower. Sadly, to close the show I had booked a comedian from Birmingham, who in true thespian parlance, 'died'. After a few minutes, he gave up the ghost. 'I'm not following him again,' the comedian stated. I had some sympathy, but he still pocketed his fee before he headed for the station.

Back to the train journey, Jackie told me that in the early fifties, he was on about £8 a week at Manchester United. After paying for his digs and sending a couple of quid home to his mum there wasn't a lot left for champagne and caviar. Another young star at Old Trafford was Yorkshireman Tommy Taylor, who knew that Jack was a tough lad, and suggested that he might be interested in the 'fight game'? Jack asked what he had in mind and Tommy told him of the illegal bouts that took place in West Yorkshire in pubs on a Monday night. 'You can get a tenner a fight.' This sounded good so Jackie went with Tommy and had a bout near Wakefield. He got his £10 but at training the next morning was sporting a nasty cut eye and a few bruises. After the session, the trainer came up to him, 'Jackie, how did you get that cut?' 'Well, I bumped into a goal post.' Nothing more was said. A week later they were off across the Pennines again, and another tenner went in Jackie's pocket, though he took a few punches. The next day the trainer called him over again, 'Jackie, I see another cut. What happened?' 'I bumped into Tommy, you know how hard he is.' The trainer then made the vital statement, 'Jackie, I wouldn't like to see any more scrapes, or Matt will have to be made aware of your "accidents", understand?' 'I certainly did and that was the end of my boxing career.'

He did say that Tommy Taylor had a set of wheels and was able to drive him to Yorkshire for his first fight. However, going over the top to Yorkshire was different in those days, there was no M62, and they broke down before they reached Huddersfield and had to call out the AA. The motorbike arrived and the AA man soon fixed the car. 'What was the problem,' asked Tommy. 'Shit in the carburettor,' was the reply. 'How often do I have to do that?'

Jackie was in poor health in 1998 and I went to see him in Tameside Hospital. He was very unwell and I did not think he would wake, but he opened his eyes, 'Ar, Mike good of you to come. We're doing a lunch in Milton Keynes next week aren't we?' 'Certainly are, Jack,' I said, 'See you there.' He smiled and went back to sleep. Jackie Blanchflower, soccer star and funny lovely man, passed away a few days later, on 2 September aged sixty-five.

Chapter 17

Geoffrey Boycott

Geoff Boycott signing autographs post-lunch at Sachas Hotel in Manchester, circa 1986

Yorkshire has produced many great cricketers, and I have been delighted to work with a good few of them over the years, but to become friends with two who considered themselves to be the best at their profession was special – and when they worked together it was always the recipe for a great lunch. Fred Trueman told anybody that he was the best fast bowler of all time, and Geoffrey Boycott did much the same to audiences around the UK, but of course as a batsman. Truth is they genuinely believed it.

Geoff Boycott stacked up as many enemies as he did fans, but you could never doubt his knowledge of the game, or indeed his love of it. He continues to entertain as a respected commentator.

He was often asked at lunches who was the most aggressive fast bowler that he had faced in Test matches. His answer surprised many. 'Without doubt it was West Indian Colin Croft. Croft was 6ft 7in and hated batsmen, particularly if they were English. When we were on Tour in the West Indies on one night I saw Colin having a drink in a bar. I thought I would wind him up so I sat next to him. He looked at me but did not say a word. "How are you Croftsy?" No reply. "Croftsy do you hate batsmen?" He looked at me and said, "I hate batsman." "Do you only hate batsmen?" "No, man, I hate everybody." "Do you hate your grandma?" He looked me in the eye' "I even hate her," he said, and after a pause he added, "if she is batting ..."'

Fast bowlers were a major part of Geoff's speeches – he was regularly asked was he frightened at any time ... 'Just go on to the M6 motorway, stand in the outside lane and wait until a car comes at you at eighty miles an hour. When it gets about eighteen yards away, jump out of the way! That's the sort of time you have to make up your mind whether to play or leave a ball.' That did sound scary!

Michael Parkinson is one of the most famous Yorkshiremen, his chat shows are legend and when I suggested that there could be a superb lunch if Parky interviewed Boycs, Geoffrey thought it would be a great idea, and gave me Michael's number. Luckily, he agreed and we did a couple of events.

Geoffrey's relationship with Fred Trueman was a constant source of interest to my clients, but he rarely slagged off the great fast bowler in his speeches. Indeed, he often told of being a new member of the Yorkshire first team. He said on an early appearance at Headingley, he looked around the dressing room and Fred was nowhere to be seen. 'Is Mr Trueman not playing?' he asked his teammates. One of the old pros laughed and told him to look in the visitors' dressing room – there was Fred, holding court with the younger members of the opposition. 'Now what number do tha bat?' he asked a fresh-faced youngster. 'Number 4,' came the reply. 'Good that's at least two wickets in this game.' Fred would puff on his pipe and smile, I bet they were glad to get rid of him!

Geoffrey loved his sport and was an avid Manchester United supporter. He loved going to the football version of Old Trafford, but it was golf that was his other passion. Back in the late seventies I had moved to Cheshire from Surrey but I had been involved in football for many years. It was the start of a great adventure, and ultimately led to making many friends in the world of sport, Geoffrey Boycott being one. I managed several clubs after the move north, including Bramhall in the Mid-Cheshire League.

One of my players from those early days was Dave Stewardson, who had gone on to play in the Football Conference with Stalybridge Celtic. Stewie's young son (who unfortunately died not long after) had a terrible illness and Stewie was helping a charity trying to combat the disease. So, another of my old team, David Booth, asked if I would put a golf group together for a fundraiser at Hazel Grove Golf Club.

My team of three was self, Roger Hunt (Liverpool and England World Cup winner) and Geoffrey Boycott. We were given a 2.30 tee-off time, so I pitched up about half past one, met Roger in the car park and headed for the clubhouse for a quick soup and sarnie, but no sign of 'Sir Geoffrey'. Two o'clock came and I was a little concerned. Had he gone to the wrong course? Had I told him Bramhall not Hazel Grove? Stewie came over, 'Are you looking for Geoff Boycott? He's just come off the practice area. He's been here since 11 o'clock.' That was the mark of the man, professional in everything he did not just on the cricket field.

Roger did not know Boycs so as we played the first few holes Geoff quizzed the great footballer 'What was Shankly like to play for? What about Alf Ramsey? What about playing in a World Cup Final?' They were getting on great and their golf wasn't bad either! As we walked up the sixth Roger said to Geoffrey that he hit a very good ball then he asked, 'Geoff, If you had played golf instead of cricket how do you think you would have done?' Geoff paused to hit a great five-iron onto the green, then turned to Roger and said, 'I would have won a couple of majors.' There was not a trace of irony in the comment. Roger and I just walked on and Roger whispered, 'He's not short of confidence, is he?'

Chapter 18

Willie John McBride

Left to Right – John Dawes, Colin "Pinetree" Meads and Willie John McBride. Three of the greatest Rugby Union Captains

Not many rugby players did or will ever play on five Lions tours. W. J. McBride, MBE, of Ballymena and Ireland, went on five tours and famously captained the greatest tour of all, to South Africa in 1974. He went on to manage another tour and coach Ireland for an unhappy year, forced out by rugby politics, a shabby way for their former captain to be treated. It left a sore wound on the 'big man' as Broonie called him, but he went on to be one of the most inspirational and amusing speakers I have had the pleasure to work with and the privilege to call my friend.

Willie John's career in the green jersey ended at Cardiff where Ireland had been heavily walloped by a great Wales team that included the likes of Gareth Edwards, J. P. R. Williams, Gerald

Davies, Phil Bennett, Merv 'the swerve' Davies and the Pontypool front row. If you are going to finish, and lose, they were one of the best sides ever to lose to. It was the Ireland centenary year to boot, so Willie John. was not happy as he packed his bag, and left the dressing room. On his way out he encountered a couple of Irish supporters who had obviously had a drink or three, and were having trouble finding the exit. They saw Willie John and one of them greeted the great man, 'Ah, Willie John, I know it's the centenary of the Union, but you sure didn't have to play like one of the fecking founder members.' 'Yep, it was time to retire,' thought Willie John. He played on for Ballymena until he was forty, but then he decided it was time to go when a young buck from an opposing side took too many liberties and 'I belted him.' This time the boots went in the cupboard, not to be used again as a player.

Willie John was a feared opponent. Fergus Slattery remembered a call during a battle against the enemy England, 'Kick ahead, kick any fecking head,' but Willie John denied making that call, 'I was hard but never dirty.' Some might say some of the punch ups with the Springboks in 1974 might have told another story. His famous call of '99' is legend and has been recalled by Broonie in this book. Willie John told me that the call was really to have been '999' to bring all players to the aid of their comrades, but 999 took too long to say and it became, 'When I shout 99 you hit the nearest opponent to you.'

When I ran a reunion for the 1974 Tour in 2004, the whole squad turned up at the Grosvenor House in London. We had lost 'Broon from Troon' in 2000, but every player seemed to have a story about their leader and many of them related to a famous night in Pretoria, where the Lions won the Second Test 28–9, to put them 2–0 up in the series. Back in the hotel, Willie John shocked the squad by announcing his retirement as captain adding 'until Monday morning'. This gave rise to mayhem. 'I remember lying in my underpants with the room doing circles aware that there was banging on my door. There were Roger

Uttley and Mervyn Davies, both of them pissed, "You'd better come, there's a bit of trouble." I picked up my pipe – it was 3 a.m. – and followed them into what looked like a war zone. When I saw Bobby Windsor with a fire hose, I sobered up pretty quickly.' The hotel manager was going berserk, and the Lions were not helping. Willie John, still in only his pants, told the irate manger that he was captain of the team and asked what was the problem? By now the manager was at the end of his tether and said, 'That's it, I've had enough, I'm getting the Pretoria police,' and went to press the lift button. Willie John said, 'Excuse me, do you think there will be many of them?' The manager stopped as the Lions cheered. 'That was bloody good,' he said to the captain. Willie John said that the boys were pissed, but that he would get them off to bed. They would sort out the mess next morning, which they did, and a few hundred rand fixed what could have been an international scandal. What a captain.

The players all remembered that night, though two other incidents from Pretoria came to Willie John's mind. It was on the way to the ground for the Test that Billy Steele, the Scotland winger, got the players to sing 'Flower of Scotland'. It became the Scottish National Anthem (this was before it was adopted as the Scottish rugby anthem) and the players sang with gusto. They would not get off the team bus at the ground until 'Flower' had been completed.

The other incident was as they were about to leave the hotel. A very angry red-faced manager of the Lions, Alan Thomas, got on the bus. 'Which of you buggers has been in my room and phoned the UK?' Not a soul moved. 'OK I will have to expose the culprit myself. The number phoned was Pontypool 31748.' Up jumped Bobby Windsor. 'Which one of you bastards has been phoning my wife?' Nobody ever knew if Alan Thomas got the 1,500 rand that the calls cost from Bobby.

Chapter 19

Ian Robertson and memories of Bill McLaren

Left to Right – Bill McLaren, Guest of Reuters, Gordon Brown and Ian Robertson

I have many reasons to be grateful to 'Robbo' not least that through his friendship with Nigel Wray he instigated the sale of MBN Promotions in 2005. Ian and I go back well over thirty years and he introduced me to many of the greatest names in rugby union. In turn, I was able to use him as a speaker, interviewer, auctioneer at every MBN venue, some (like the Grosvenor House) on many occasions. Ian has been the BBC Radio 'Voice of Rugby' since Obolensky was a lad, and to date has written forty-eight books, mainly on rugby, but also a famous biography of the legendary actor Richard Burton. In all our years together we have never had a written contract. We would discuss a project, I would agree to buy cartloads of books for the lunches and after the dust had settled on an event we would attempt to recall the 'deal' we had agreed and the fee. I would drive my team at MBN mad as we tried to remember the Robbo arrangement. Money would change hands and everybody was happy.

Ian would not like me to tell you this, but over the years he has raised enormous sums of money for his charity projects, not least for the rugby charity Wooden Spoon. I well remember that for the British Lions of 1974 reunion lunch in London in 2004 we produced some rugby shirts that were signed by the whole squad, with Broonie's signature woven into the shirt by Fran Cotton's company Cotton Traders. At the end of the event, after giving all the players a shirt to remember the day, a number were taken by Robbo for the Wooden Spoon, and they raised a large sum for the charity that year.

One of the characters he introduced me to was England's most capped front-row forward and British Lion Jason Leonard. Robbo said that there were not too many Mensa members from the front-row union and on one occasion Robbo, a fierce Scot, was rubbishing England, as he often did using, as commentators often do, statistics. Jason, a patriotic Englishman, protested and riposted to Ian, 'We might be rubbish now Robbo, but soon we will arise from the ashes like a pheasant.' Back came Robbo, 'Don't you mean a phoenix?' 'Oh yeah I knew it was some fancy bird beginning with F.'

A book that Robbo did not produce was my *Reuters' Century of Great British Sport*. Harper Collins were the publishers and I collaborated with journalist Tim Collings. News giants Reuters helped me produce a book for the millennium that accompanied a series of my sporting lunches. Many star names appeared and Ian helped me host the events. Reuters sponsored the top table at each lunch, and their man in charge of looking after clients was Adrian Duffield, a big rugby fan. Robbo has a wicked sense of humour and decided that Adrian was ripe for a bit of teasing. 'Reuters are a caring company and look after their staff who work so hard for them. Adrian Duffield is one such man, and last year, his caring employer decided that Adrian needed a break.

So, they sent him to Australia for a period of R&R. He got a car in Sydney, with instructions to get to a holiday bungalow deep in the outback. There was little about, except kangaroos, when he came across a farmer by the roadside. Adrian introduced himself as an executive of that caring company Reuters, and did the Aussie know where the bungalow was. 'I do, mate. It's about forty miles up the road, and I'm your next-door neighbour.' Adrian thanked him and as he was about to go the farmer asked if he would like to drive over that evening for a barbeque. 'What will there be?' asked Adrian, 'Well, cobber, there will be giant prawns, as big as your hand, steaks, lots of beer, and loads of sex, then more beer and lots more sex.' 'That sounds great – what shall I wear?' 'Wear what you like, mate, there will only be the two of us ...'

Adrian got that at every lunch, including one in London in the company of his chairman. He survived but I don't know if he is still in touch with his Aussie pal!

I doubt whether the first story Robbo told at one of my events would get pass the P.C. brigade but it was very funny. It went back to his days as a student in Aberdeen. He shared rooms with a psychic who one day told him that he knew that the following morning, at 9 a.m. precisely; the Pope was going to die. 'Right. get your coat. We're off to Ladbrokes in Union Street.' When they got there Robbo asked the manager for the odds on his Holiness the Pope passing away at 9 o'clock the next day? 'We don't bet on that,' was the manager's reply. 'Oh but Ladbrokes will take a bet on any event.' 'Right oh,' he was told, 'I'll go and check'. When he came back he said 500–1, not great odds thought Robbo, but they put a tenner on it and as they left the bookies Robbo saw an old man who looked down on his luck. He went over and whispered the news of the pontiff's demise to the old man, 'Go and fill your boots.' 'Thank you son, you're a real Christian.' Next morning, on the news, came the sad news that at 9 a.m. his Holiness the Pope had passed away. 'Excellent let's get down to Ladbrokes and collect.' As they left with their winnings Robbo saw the old man. 'Did you have a bet?' 'I did son but you know when your luck's out. Sadly, I did him in a double with the Archbishop of Canterbury!'

Ian, as I said earlier introduced me to some great rugby men. Not least that doyen of commentators Bill McLaren. We went up to Hawick, Bill's home town in the Borders, and met with him and his delightful wife Bette. Our plan was to ask him to do a few MBN lunches. Now it was a fact that Bill had steadfastly refused hundreds of requests to speak at events. 'I could not do that son, have a Hawick mint ball.' Bill was very fond of Robbo, however, and after much persuasion from Robbo he amazingly agreed. My only input was to confirm the fee and the deal was done. Even the great Ian Robertson was surprised and we had some very happy events.

Our first was in Aberdeen and a round of golf at the Royal Aberdeen course preceded the lunch the day before. Bill was in his seventies but was a very canny player. Robbo loves his golf, and I made up the three-ball. Bill wound me up after I had hit one particularly long drive with, 'I don't go that far on my holidays son.' I soon reverted to my usual brand of good, bad and downright ugly, and only a thick sea fog got us to call the match a draw. It could have been expensive. Next day, at the Copthorne Hotel, Bill gave his first speech. If we had any worries that he would 'freeze' he soon settled that and I hope he even started to enjoy the events. Our happiest day was at the lovely Sheraton Grand Hotel in Edinburgh city centre where Bette and other members of the McLaren clan gathered with nearly 500 guests to hear him tell many happy stories of his life in rugby and the BBC. The only shadow on the proceedings was the battle with cancer being fought by his lovely daughter Janey. You would never have known it, as she beamed up at her dad as he spoke.

Janey did not beat the dreaded disease and it hit Bette and Bill very hard. That Christmas a parcel arrived from Bill, it was a

Hawick green Pringle sweater. I wore it for years and only let it go when Doreen could not patch the holes any more.

I spoke to Robbo shortly after Bill passed away on 19 January 2010 at the age of eighty-six in his beloved Hawick. Not long before he died, Robbo went up to see him at home. Bette said he was very poorly and might well not recognise his old friend. Robbo was greeted by that famous voice 'I. Robertson, Cambridge University, Watsonians, London Scottish, Barbarians, 8 caps for Scotland, couldn't kick and never tackled …' Spot on as ever.

Broon from Troon was another of our great friends and Robbo was perhaps a tad envious of the big man's fabulous speeches – they were very competitive to say the least. We were at one of Robbo's fundraising dinners where Gordon was due to speak. A delayed flight meant he was very late and Robbo stepped in to do twenty minutes while we waited for Broonie. During his speech Robbo told one of Broonie's famous line out stories, and told it so well, it got the biggest laugh of the night. Robbo, as you will have gathered, can be a very bad man. So, he told the audience that when Gordon arrived he was bound to tell the story and would no one laugh or smile. Broonie arrived and promptly told the line out story, to complete silence and not a smile. Broonie looked at Robbo, obviously nonplussed, so thinking he had got it wrong, promptly told it again with even more gusto. Total silence. He managed to get back on track and finish and it was not until an audience member gave the game away in the bar afterwards that he realised that he had been had. Robbo made a run for it or he might not have been in a fit state to speak at any more of my events.

Robbo 'got' me on occasion but was always careful, after all I was the paymaster. He would turn up at a lunch with the usual greeting, 'No show without Punch.' Did he mean me or him? I never knew.

However, I did get him, only once. It was at a lunch to celebrate thirty years after the Lions had beaten New Zealand in

1971. Captain John Dawes from Wales was guest of honour and many of my usual suspects were to speak. Willie John, Gareth Edwards, Fergus Slattery and David Duckham plus Robbo to link the show. As I got up to introduce Robbo I went through his CV and finished with, 'And Ian was in the running to make the tour party to New Zealand in 1971, but sadly missed out due to a serious lack of ability.' It brought the house down, but Robbo punched me on the arm as he got up. 'I do the jokes,' were his words. But it was lovely!

121

Chapter 20

'Ossie'

Left to Right – Steve Kindon, Peter Osgood, Dave Mackay, Mike Newlin, Matt Le Tissier and Paul Fletcher. Taken at the Grosvenor House in London. Spurs and Scotland's legendary Captain Dave Mackay was Guest of Honour with our four great speakers

Peter Osgood was one of Chelsea's greatest. At times he was a maverick, who upset England managers and so never won nearly enough caps for his country. But watching him play, as I did, was always fun and boy was he a goal-scorer. A poll by supporters had him at number one, something that made him very proud.

One of Ossie's best pals was a striker who should have had a long career at Stamford Bridge, but injuries and illness counted against him, and Ian Hutchinson died in 2002, sadly at the early age of fifty-four. Ian joined Chelsea from Cambridge United and, as well as being a top striker, he will always be remembered for his long throw-ins, one of which helped win the FA Cup in 1970 when David Webb scored the winner against Leeds United in the final replay. Ossie recalls one day when Chelsea were due to play Nottingham Forest. Ian was looking worried about the game and confided in his co-striker that he was very concerned about coming up against an old enemy, Sammy Chapman. 'I played against him when I was at Burton Albion, and he's a right handful.' True to form Chapman clattered 'Hutch' early on and cut him above the eye. At half time, Ossie told Ian that he should get his own back. The plan was that early in the second half, when Chelsea got a corner, Oz would take out the Forest goalkeeper, Peter Grummitt, and, while the referee sorted it out, Ian should whack Chapman (no cameras in those days), so no one would notice. It worked like a dream, and while Ossie was rolling on the floor with Grummitt, there was a crack and howl, and when sanity was restored Ian called over to Ossie, 'He's broken me f****** arm now.'

Chelsea was always Peter's love but after ten years at Stamford Bridge he moved to the south coast when Lawrie McMenemy signed him for Southampton. 'In fact, I was kidnapped by Lawrie Mac, he invited me to his house, locked the door and told me I could not leave until I signed for the club. Now Lawrie was a very big bloke, so what could I do?' He joined a club that went on to play in the FA Cup Final in 1976 and a famous 1–0 win over Tommy Docherty's Manchester United. However, before the famous final the Saints had to visit Grimsby Town for a league game. The team travelled on Friday for the long journey to the north-east. When they had checked in to their hotel, Mick Channon, that famous racehorse trainer (also not a bad player), got the players together and told them that they deserved a celebration for getting to the Cup Final. So, they were told to come to his room where he had laid on a large quantity of lager. When the players finally got to bed it was after 5 a.m. and they were very much the worse for wear. Ossie said that there is always a 'snitch' at a football club, and true to form the manager got to hear about the party and when they got into the dressing room for the game, still worse for wear, Lawrie McMenemy went absolutely mad. (I spoke to Lawrie at a lunch years later and he said that was an understatement,) His attack went something like ... 'You 'orrible bastards, you should be ashamed of yourselves. There are hundreds of our fans out there who have travelled since dawn to get here to cheer you on, and how do you repay them? You go out drinking all night and turn up pissed, shame on you,' and with that he stormed out. Oz said they all felt bad and went out to play (very badly), coming in at half time at 0–0. Lawrie's mood had not improved. 'I can't even look at you, I'm not even sure if I want to be your manager.' Channon piped up, 'Don't worry Gaffer we won't let you down.' 'You've already done that,' sighed Big Lawrie. In the second half Southampton won the match 5–0, and Mickey Channon scored four goals. As they got back to the dressing room, after a salute to the fans, the manager came in and slammed the door. 'You lucky, lucky bastards,' was all he said. 'Lucky, gaffer? If the lager hadn't run out, we would have won 9–0 no sweat.' That at least got a smile out of Mr McMenemy.

After football Ossie turned to speaking at lunches and dinners, and playing golf. He looked after corporate guests at Stamford Bridge, where a statue of him meets fans on arrival at the ground.

It was Ron 'Chopper' Harris who phoned me on 1 March 2006. Peter Osgood was attending a funeral when he had a fatal heart attack. I had seen him at the Belfry, where he was playing golf, not long before he died. He was complaining of his bad knees. Fifty-nine was too young.

125

Chapter 21

Sir Bobby Charlton

Left to Right – Comedian and TV star Tom O' Connor, Sir Bobby Charlton, Mike Newlin and Dusty Miller

It was February 1958, I was 10½ and was into football. I had watched Wolves on the television playing Honved from Hungary, so they became my team. I had not seen them 'live', but I had also followed Arsenal, so as I got home from school that cold February day, news was coming through that a plane bringing Manchester United home from a European Cup game had crashed whilst trying to take off from Munich Airport in thick snow. My shock was compounded by the fact that United had just played Arsenal in a thriller at Highbury, before they had left for Belgrade to play that quarter final. Playing at number eight was a relatively unknown fair-haired forward, in because of an injury, Robert Charlton. Much has been written and said about the crash, Bobby was injured but OK, many others did not make it, and many that did survive became important contributors to my lunches and crop up many times through these memoirs. The loss of Duncan Edwards, after he had survived the crash for a few days, was particularly poignant, and affected Bobby deeply.

Years later when we were sitting in Manchester Airport with time on our hands Bobby told us about how much Duncan had influenced him and mentioned that they had played together before United, whilst on National Service. It was at Catterick army camp in Yorkshire, and they played the RAF. Duncan ran the game, a giant on the pitch. The defining moment came when Duncan called for the ball from their keeper, passed to Bob in midfield, demanded it back, beat three RAF men as he strode upfield, and as he approached the penalty box unleashed a cannonball shot. The RAF keeper ducked – the ball was arrowing straight for his head – and the ball almost broke the net. Bobby looked at Duncan with an admiration that would last until the tragedy in Munich.

Many years later, now Sir Bobby, he was doing an ambassador's job for the FA in Cambridgeshire. He was walking down the high street in Wisbech when he got a tug on the arm. As he turned around, a grey-haired gentleman said, 'Bob, we played against each other once.' Not recognising him, Bobby asked when this was. 'It was at Catterick, I played for the RAF.' 'I remember the game very well,' Bobby told him. 'That was the game when Duncan Edwards hit a shot so hard the opposing goalkeeper ducked.' 'Yes, that was me – it was the proudest moment of my life!'

I first met Sir Bob in 1980, when my lunches in Manchester were proving very popular. I had met a real Manchester character, Freddie Pye, who ran a scrap metal business, and was chairman of Wigan Athletic. Bobby was on the board of the club, and we were introduced at a game. I cheekily asked Bob if he would do my lunch in Manchester, and he agreed. No fee, but he and Fred did not have to pay for their chicken dinner! What a good day we had and Sir Bobby went on to speak at many of my events over many years. However, the fees were significantly higher, and he was worth every penny.

I have had the pleasure in knowing the Charltons very well – both Bobby and Jack spoke for me on dozens of occasions. Much has been made of the supposed feud between the brothers. Knowing my involvement, many journalists used to ring me for gossip – not a chance! I liked them both and as in football what goes on in the dressing room stays there. What I will tell you is that I asked them both to speak at a 'Boys of 66' lunch at the Grosvenor House in 2001 to celebrate to celebrate thirty-five years since the World Cup win – any excuse for a party! Jack was easy, one phone call and his response was, as always, 'I'll look in me book.' Then I broached the subject of speaking with his kid brother as he called Bobby. No problem with me was Jack's response. So on to Sir Bob. We met for a coffee in the Four Seasons Hotel in Hale, and I told Bobby the idea of the Boys of 66 reunion lunch in London, and who had already agreed to attend. I then tackled the 64,000-dollar question: would he speak along with Jack? No problem with me was also Bob's response. Deal done I left a happy man.

Chapter 22

Lisbon Lions

Left to Right – Wilf McGuinness (Coach of Manchester United in 1968), Sean Fallon (Coach of Celtic FC in 1967), John Aston (Manchester United), Sir Bobby Charlton (Manchester United), Tommy Gemmell (Celtic FC), Mike Newlin, Bill Foulkes (Manchester United), Paddy Crerand (Manchester United and Ex-Celtic FC), Ronnie Simpson (Celtic FC), David Sadler (Manchester United), Steve Chalmers (Celtic FC), Billy McNeill (Captain of Celtic FC in 1967), Alex Stepney (Manchester United), Bobby Lennox (Celtic FC), Bertie Auld (Celtic FC), Tony Dunne (Manchester United).
This is a unique reunion of the Celtic European Cup Winners in 1967, and Manchester United, winners in 1968. No British teams had won the European Cup until the Lions in 1967.

My Glasgow lunches had become very popular. It is a fabulous City with a vibrant business community but I was always aware of the tensions between the Catholic Green side of the City and the Protestant Blue. I always found sportsmen were just 'people' and early on I put on a lunch in Glasgow featuring the Rangers great - Jim Baxter. 'Slim Jim' was his nickname [he had put on a pound or two since he retired!] I also invited to speak, Celtic's Jimmy Johnstone, known as 'Jinky' for his brilliant dribbling skills on the wing. I must admit one or two people thought the idea was ambitious!

Thankfully it was a superb day and over 400 guests cheered them at the end. I was proud to have brought the two sides together! In the Green Room after the lunch the two scallywags got me horribly drunk on brandy - but that is another tale.

In later years, I got to know Jim Craig, who played right-back for Celtic in Lisbon. 'Cairney' as he was called by his teammates was called 'posh' because of his University education, and he went on to become a successful Dentist after football. Jim was an accomplished speaker and his book, 'A Lion looks back', showed a deep knowledge of the history of the great club. Our friendship led to a reunion lunch of the Lisbon Lions in the Glasgow Thistle in 1997. Every team member attended and was introduced with affectionate stories by 'Cairney'. Sadly, only Willie Wallace could not make it due to the fact he lives in Australia.

In the Sponsors bar before the event I had been puzzled by the players all calling goalkeeper Ronnie Simpson 'Father'. Jim explained in his speech that that Ronnie was called 'Father', because he was so old in 1967. Ronnie was 36 (!) and refused to play in his dentures (Jim did make it clear he was not Ron's dentist!). He said that it was a bonus because Ron would shout at Jim all the time - but he could not understand a word with the keeper's teeth out!! Ronnie Simpson had been a star for Newcastle United and played in the 1952 and 1955 FA Cup Finals at Wembley.

I took 'Father' to a lunch in his honour at the Forte Hotel in Newcastle. They loved him, and standing ovations were the norm. George Best reckoned Simpson was one of the great goalkeepers. If you get a chance watch Scotland v Northern Ireland in the early seventies, 'Father' was nearer 40 than 30.

When Ronnie died in April 2004, I drove up to Edinburgh for the funeral. As we left the church, the Lions were all on a coach and as I walked past, Billy McNeill kindly dashed over to ask me to join them for the wake. I had to get back to Altrincham, but appreciated the offer, and waved to a great bunch of guys. It was also the last time I saw Jinky, who was very unwell. He always called me 'big man', using that fantastic Glaswegian lilt.

Billy McNeill was the Lions and Scotland Captain. He went on to be a top-class manager, and when he managed Manchester City he lived close to me in Cheshire. To Celtic he was 'Ceaser' and 30 years on he was still the leader. He liked a beer and chat and loved his golf, but to the band of brothers that are the Lisbon Lions, he will always be 'Ceaser'. At the time of writing Billy is suffering from dementia – opening up the discussion of whether heading so many footballs in his long career as a centre half, may have contributed to his condition?

Chapter 23

The Boys of 66 Reunion Lunch 2001

35 years on from their 1966 glory, the squad reunited, sadly missing their Captain Bobby Moore. Can you name each player?

The Grosvenor House was the venue for our reunion lunch in 2001 for the greatest win in the history of English football. Bobby and Jack had agreed to speak together but just look at the supporting cast! Goalkeeper Gordon Banks, right back George Cohen, left back Ramon Wilson, midfield Nobby Stiles, Alan Ball, Martin Peters, strikers Roger Hunt and Geoff Hurst and trainer Wilf McGuinness. Add BBC commentator Kenneth Wolstenholme, he of 'There are some people on the pitch, they think it's all over. It is now,' as Geoff Hurst banged in the fourth goal. Only one person would have made it the greatest event of all time, the late, great Bobby Moore.

Well over a thousand guests gave every speaker and all the team standing ovations. I can still recall some of the stories:-

Gordon Banks:

'I was very proud of the 1966 win and to go on to play in the Finals in Mexico in 1970. It is probably 1970 against Brazil that I am remembered for, when I made a great save from a Pele header. Do you know that people still come up to me today and ask how I am keeping? I broke more bones in my career than I would like to recall and a car accident saw the loss of one eye, so they then ask me if I am still playing!'

Martin Peters or 'the wingless wonder', who Sir Alf said was ten years ahead of his time:

'I spend lots of time with Geoff Hurst. We don't discuss the match very often, but everyone we meet does. They always ask about the hat-trick, and the goal that bounced yards over the line. Do they ask about my goal? Very rarely. But do you realise that if Weber had not equalised for the West Germans just before ninety minutes to send us into extra time, I would have scored the winning goal in the World Cup. Was I pleased that Hursty got the winner and a hat trick to boot?'

Wilf McGuinness, trainer in the weeks leading up to the finals:

'The ball was yards over the line for our third goal, I asked Roger Hunt, 'It was a yard over,' he told me. Mind you it did look a bit closer when I saw it on the telly.'

Alan Ball:

'My dad was based up north, he was my biggest critic, and my biggest fan. I phoned him on Friday night, "Have you made the team?" "I don't know, dad. Alf hasn't named the team yet." "Well ring me as soon as he does because I'm not spending money on petrol and driving to Wembley if you're not in the team." "Thanks, dad." Well as soon as I knew, I was in, I phoned him, "Righto, I'm on my way," was all he said. I hope I made him proud.'

There are many more stories from that lunch, and some are in other chapters of this book. But I wonder if we shall ever see a team like the Boys of 66 again?

Chapter 24

Tom Burke – Muhammad Ali's Corner Man

In the early eighties, the lunches were gathering increased audiences, and we had outgrown the Brahms and Liszt pub. I moved to a famous old gentlemen's club, the Manchester Club, at the top of King Street, a famous old building. Amazingly Granada television did a documentary on the men's urinals! As women were now attending, I presumed that there had to be a Ladies cloakroom? There was!

Chay Blyth, who had rowed the Atlantic, came up from Plymouth to speak. He told an incredulous crowd that when he agreed to row the Atlantic, with one colleague, he had never been in a rowing boat before. He arrived at Boston Harbor before his co-rower, and was asked to do some promo photos for the American press. This was problematic, as he did not know how to turn the boat round, so as he went further out to sea and they had to launch the coastguard cutter to tow him back. Other great names came along, until a fateful day when the phone rang in my office. 'Hello, I am Tom Burke and I was Muhammad Ali's corner man. Can I come and see you?' You bet he could and he told me an amazing story, though now I look back on it I'm not sure how much of it was true!

Tom (he said) had been a taxi driver, doing the airport run in Manchester. One evening he picked up a fare to go to the Hotel Piccadilly in the city centre. As sometimes happens the passenger was up for a chat and the subject got on to boxing. The passenger told Tom that he was promoting a young heavyweight, who was a real prospect for a world title. He went on to ask Tom if he was involved in the fight game. Tom told him that he had spent time at the Ardwick boxing club. Tom was chatting to a man who would become world famous as the manager of Cassius Clay, AKA Muhammad Ali. Angelo Dundee it was, and he asked Tom as they arrived at the hotel if he would be interested in working in the corner for Clay. Tom said he would and they exchanged addresses. He dropped off Dundee, and thought no more of it. However, weeks later, a letter arrived from the States with a ticket to Boston and some money. Tom went to America, and for eight years was Muhammad Ali's corner man. After his time with Ali finished he went on to work with another World Champ, the legendary Roberto Duran. He then came home and bought a fish and chip shop in Rochdale! What a story, could he speak at the Manchester Club for me? Wow, the date was agreed and he turned up with (I hoped) a fund of boxing stories.

Well, dear reader, I shall try to recall how Mr Burke addressed over 200 guests.

'Ladies and gentlemen; I am very proud to be speaking to you in this historic room. I am a boy from Ardwick, and my mum and dad, would have loved to see me here.' There was a collective 'aaah' from the audience. Now Tom tell us about Ali …

'Have you heard the one about the nun who f***** the bishop?'

They had not, and looking at his notes I saw that the next jokes got progressively worse. Silence can be deafening and Tom realised that he might just have misjudged the crowd. He did at least have the good sense to sit down. As the audience departed, still no wiser about Muhammad Ali, I realised that this was not Tom's, or indeed my, finest hour. I am delighted to tell you that I was forgiven eventually and I was helped along the way by two of football's greatest, Sir Matt Busby and Joe Mercer.

Chapter 25

Sir Matt and Joe Mercer

Left to Right – Sir Tom Finney, Gordon Taylor (Chairman of the PFA), Joe Mercer and Tommy Docherty. This was taken at the Hotel Piccadilly, 27th April 1987.

After the disappointment of the Tom Burke lunch, I wanted to have a really good event at the Manchester Club. Who was the most famous name in football in Manchester? Sir Matt Busby perhaps? Martin Edwards, the United chairman, gave me Sir Matt's home number. I was aware that the great man was not keen at speaking at events, so I rang Joe Mercer, who was very good, and told him of my idea to get him and Matt to do the lunch together. He thought it was a great plan, they were very good pals. Sir Matt agreed very readily. Both men arrived about 11.30 so we had a pot of tea. They chatted as old mates do, but to my amazement they included me in the chat, as if we were all old friends. It totally relaxed me. Over 300 guests, a full house, greeted our legends with a standing ovation, and rose again as I introduced Sir Matt to speak. Everyone had said Matt would not speak, but he did. He spoke of his love of Manchester and of United and particularly of his pal Joe. Blimey! Three standing ovations and a fourth as he left the room. Joe, who famously managed Manchester City and briefly England, was a fine player with Everton and Arsenal and his speech earned him three 'standings'. At the end, he joked that United had therefore won 4–3. So, they all got up again, an honourable draw!

Two things came out of that lunch. Joe told a story during his speech. But he then started to tell the same tale, only to break off and quietly asked me, had he already told the story? I thought quickly and told him to carry on. He got a great laugh and at the end he thanked me. Sadly, it was the beginning of his descent into the dreaded Alzheimer's. He stopped speaking but I kept in touch with his wife and he came to several lunches and was always popular until he passed away in 1990.

139

Chapter 26

Kevin Keegan and a little bit of Denis Law

M B N   P R O M O T I O N S
present

LUNCHEON
with

Kevin Keegan

at the Forte Crest, Newcastle-Upon-Tyne
on Thursday 24th March 1994

Sponsored by

Grant Thornton

A souvenir menu from the lunch. Kevin had not long been appointed manager of Newcastle United,
which ensured a sell-out crowd at the Forte Crest Hotel!

Newcastle on Tyne was one of the toughest venues for my lunches. Our venue was the Forte Crest Hotel in the city centre. It was staffed by lovely people; the food was good and the waitresses and waiters were great. However, the audience were a tough lot! I took Denis Law on one occasion and during his speech he whispered to me, 'What am I getting wrong, they're not laughing?' I assured him that they were paying the best of attention, but had to admit to feeling a little hot under the collar myself. Denis sat down to thunderous applause. 'Told you so,' I said a little smugly, but also relieved. As he signed for the autograph queue, one guest said, 'That was great, canny lad, best speech I've heard.' Denis smiled and signed his menu. 'Tell me – why didn't you bloody laugh then?'

Well everything changed on 24 March 1994. Our special guest was the manager of Newcastle United, Kevin Keegan, who, as far as most Geordies were concerned in those days, could walk across the River Tyne to Gateshead, and not need the bridges! We could not fit another body in the banqueting room, well over 400 guests, and we could probably have sold the same again. As Kevin arrived the hotel concierge Alan Brown, who did a similar job at St James's Park on match days, met the 'Boss' and parked his car. As I took Kevin to the sponsor's room, he asked a favour. Could I arrange for a telephone line to be available at top table? No problem, I told him. 'Thanks, we are in the middle of a transfer deal and I've left Terry McDermott in charge of the negotiation.' It turned out that the player concerned was the Coventry City centre half Phil Babb. While we were eating the phone rang – it was Terry at the ground. He told Kevin that a transfer fee had been agreed with Coventry. 'How much is he looking for in wages?' Terry told him. 'How much?!' Terry told him again, 'Tell him to go home.' With that Kevin put the phone down and got up to apologise to the whole audience, telling them the outcome, I think it must be unique that a transfer discussion was made at an MBN lunch.

Kevin was a great player. He became a legend at Hamburg and for England, but it was at Anfield that he played his best football and the Scousers loved him. Well the red ones did. When the time came to leave Lawrie McMenemy managed to persuade him to join Southampton – just like he had Peter Osgood. Kevin knew he was committing himself to a club with big ambitions but when the league match at Anfield came along he was very excited and told anyone prepared to listen how much he loved the Liverpool fans. When the team coach arrived, they cheered Kevin as he got off the bus, and he signed autographs before going into the dressing room. After the game (Liverpool won 2–0) the manager asked the players to get on the coach as soon as possible as it was a long journey home. As Kevin emerged there was still a big crowd of Liverpool fans outside and he went over to sign and have photos with them. Lawrie shouted for Kevin to board, but he said, 'These are my people,' and carried on signing. Finally, Lawrie got Kevin on board, 'Gaffer they're my people. I had to see them.' Some of the players were starting a card school for the trip and asked Kevin if he was playing. He was and as he joined them he went to get his money out. 'Those Scouse bastards have nicked me wallet!'

143

Chapter 27

Billy Wright and Joy Beverley

Twins Teddie and Babs wish good luck to the third of the singing Beverley Sisters, Joy, on her marriage to England and Wolverhampton football captain Billy Wright.
copyright to PA Images

Why, at the age of eight, I became a Wolverhampton Wanderers supporter, I am not sure. It was probably seeing them on our first television set playing Hungary's champion club Honved, under the lights at Molineux. Although in black and white it was magical and I went to school and did a project on the Wolves and followed every result on 'Sports Report' on Saturday afternoons. So, move on over forty years and I am on the phone to their great captain Billy Wright. He was England captain too, and won over 100 caps, the first player to do so, and also he managed the

Arsenal. 'Would you come and speak at a lunch for me in London?' I asked. 'I would be delighted. Can I bring my wife along?' So it was that I met Joy Beverley, the eldest of the famous Beverley Sisters. It was a good event. Billy would never have won a comedy prize as a speaker but he was a lovely man and everyone warmed to him. I sat next to Joy and we got on like a house on fire. She had obviously been quite a girl – they were the Beckhams of their era. As I got to know them, Joy later paid me the great compliment of asking if I would organise a reunion tour for the 'Beverleys'. Sadly MBN had become so busy that I had to decline but I saw that the following year the tour took place. Billy passed away and Joy and I lost touch but it had been fun.

Knowing that I was a Wolves supporter, Billy used to invite me to home games. On my first visit, he took me up to a box in the new stand and said that the club were to name a stand after him. 'I have to meet the corporate guests with another great Wanderer Peter Broadbent (more of him in the Wilf McGuinness chapter) so would you look after my old friend?' indicating an elderly gentleman sitting in the box. 'Delighted' I told him and I sat next to his friend and introduced myself. 'Stanley' was all he said in reply. Can you believe it was Wolves' most famous manager, Stan Cullis? What a privilege. He told me tales of the great days in the 1950s. Not least that the Wolves used to love playing in the mud, so even in September he used to get the local fire brigade to practice on the pitch on Fridays and flood the ground. Teams would turn up on sunny Saturdays to play in ankle-deep gloop. Imagine Arsenal turning up at Old Trafford and finding those conditions today? He also told me that his trainer used to get the players to take a pill to pep them up if needed. I asked Billy later what the pills were, 'Polo mints' he said. You can't doubt the great Billy Wright! I still have to pinch myself when I think of all the great players and managers I have met. Years later when I had a season as commercial director of Rochdale, I went to a League game at Molineux. No great names any more, but a few ghosts.

145

Chapter 28

Geoffrey 'Dusty' Miller

Left to Right – Mike Watkinson (Lancashire player and coach, England cricketer and brilliant speaker), Mike Newlin and Dusty

Geoff Miller, Dusty to everyone, had a long and successful cricketing career. He played for Derbyshire and captained them for several seasons. An off-spin bowler and batsman he was good enough to play in twenty-seven Test matches for England and at the end of his career he spent a couple of years at Essex. He also reached the position of chairman of selectors for the English Cricket Board but since we met he has become one of the very best speakers at my lunches.

He used to say that he was a very boring cricketer. He did have twenty-seven tests, but only two were positive!

Since he came from Derbyshire they hated him in Yorkshire. He recalled attending a dinner at Wombwell Cricket Society, which he thought went very well. At the end of the event an older guest, obviously a local, came up to the top table. 'That was very good, lad. I really enjoyed that. I can tell thee that I've watched you play for twenty years and can tell you that you've given me more pleasure in the last half hour than you did in all those years.'

'The Yorkies really did not like me but I thought they would relent when I took my fiftieth test wicket. It was at Headingley against the West Indies and of all people I clean bowled the great Viv Richards. At the end of the over I made my way to field near the infamous Western Terrace, and I expected some applause. Instead one voice greeted me with, 'Oi Miller, you tosser. I've just paid twenty quid to watch Viv Richards bat!'

In 1978 Geoff toured Australia and faced one of the greatest Aussie fast bowlers, Dennis Lillee. 'I hate Australians; I get up an hour early to hate them a bit longer. If you want to know the difference between Aussies and New Zealanders ask a Kiwi if he would make love to a fourteen-year-old. He would say don't be disgusting. Ask an Aussie the same question and he'll say, 'A fourteen-year-old what?'

Towards the end of a day's play, Geoff Boycott and Mike Brearley were playing for the close and Dusty was the nominated night watchman if a wicket fell. Boycs got out and Dusty went out and saw it through to the finish with Brearley. Next morning, they resumed and did well, Lillee wasn't trying to kill them and seemed in a docile mood. Brearley then got out and, walking to the wicket with his bat over his shoulder and singing 'The Sun Has Got His Hat On' was the madman from Nottinghamshire, Derek Randall. 'Not bowling too quick today, Dennis. Were you on the nest last night?' Lillee moved his mark back another ten yards, and as Derek took his guard he looked at the rotund figure of Rodney Marsh, the Aussie wicket-keeper, about twenty yards behind the stumps and spoke – 'Hey Marshie, Santa Claus isn't coming to our house this Christmas, you've eaten him, you fat bastard.' Never upset the Aussies, so Dusty got out quickly – good decision!

Dusty thought a number of his colleagues in the Derby side were also mad and two in particular stood out for him. Fred Swarbrook was a left arm spin bowler, who got the cricketing equivalent of golf's 'yips'. He could not pitch the ball and frightened wicket-keeper Bob Taylor with a series of full tosses. It became so bad that Dusty got him to see a psychologist, whose suggestion was that Fred should carry a stone in his pocket, and when he was asked to bowl, he should rub the stone, not the ball, then try to bowl. First ball went past the batsman's head, almost taking out Bob Taylor and going for four byes. Dusty went over to Fred – 'Fred lad, try rubbing the ball and bowling the stone.' He did recover eventually.

Derby also had a Danish fast bowler – Ole Mortenson. 'Stan' to everyone after the Blackpool and England centre forward. He was a good player, who unfortunately suffered from a terrible stammer. 'What did you do before you became a cricketer' asked Dusty. 'I u u u sed to s s sell bibles.' 'Did you sell many, Stan?' 'Lots, I u u sed to knock on the d d d oor, and say w w would you like to b b buy a b b bible, or s s should I r r read it to you?'

Dusty found a clinic in London that treated stammering and went to London with him. They got a taxi and the driver said, 'Where to, mate?' Stan said, 'The c c clinic for s s s stamerrers.' 'You don't need to go there, you're bloody good at it,' was the driver's reply.

Dusty was a good friend of the legend that was Ian Botham. They used to room together on England tours. 'Well I say roomed together, when I was in 'Both' was out, and if he did come back, I was watching in the wardrobe!' So, we hatched a plan for a series of Botham and Miller lunches. After one lunch in Bristol, Beefy went home with Dusty as we were in Leeds the following day. As they got to Derby they called in to a supermarket as a few bottles of wine were needed for dinner. As they went up the drinks aisle with a shopping trolley for the booze, Beefy's mobile phone started to bleep. A customer called over to his mate, 'Look out the fat bastard's reversing.'

Both's wine-drinking exploits were legendary and his tastes were expensive. When we were discussing the tour of lunches, Dusty and I met up with Ian and his wife Cath for dinner, before a Test at the Oval. Michael Holding joined us and we went to a nice Italian, close to the ground. When it came to ordering the wine Both took charge, and the order was looking like costing several hundred pounds. When he went for a pee Dusty asked the maitre'd to decant a few bottles of the house wine, saving my credit card from a terrible hammering. Both never knew the difference and a good time was had by all. Deal done, the lunches went well. We had a visit to Belfast and were then due to fly on to Glasgow. Both announced that he had arranged for a private plane for the flight, did we want to join him? Of course we did, and arriving in Glasgow we were met by a chauffeured limo for the drive into the city. As we approached the Thistle Hotel where the following day's lunch was to take place, and where I had rooms booked for that night, Both announced that he was not going to stay at the Thistle, so we dropped him at the much smarter Malmaison Hotel, and he was not joining us for dinner either. Do you think he twigged what had happened at the Oval? How the superstars live ...

Back to cricket. Towards the end of his career, Dusty went to play for my home county Essex: 'They made me an offer I could not understand.' So, he went off to Chelmsford. If he thought Derbyshire were eccentric they were not in Essex's league. Most county sides try to complete their pre-season training with a team-bonding tour to sunny climes. Lancashire liked South Africa and others preferred the West Indies. When Dusty got to Essex the captain, Graham Gooch, proudly announced that the pre-season trip was to be to Stuttgart, West Germany. Now West Germany in March was not necessarily the players' first choice. However, they boarded the team coach, and were introduced to their driver, who was called Barry Dryer. Now one of Essex's practical jokers was one John Kenneth Lever, England fast left arm bowler and his opening gambit was 'Hello Spin.' Goochie warned him not to upset the man who was driving all the way to Stuttgart. As the journey progressed a voice from the back piped up, 'Are we nearly there yet, Tumble?' Goochie warned the perpetrator that there would be extra cross countries or at least a route march on arrival, so peace was resumed. On arrival at their hotel the players were joined at dinner by Barry and all was well until a voice came over the hotel intercom. 'Achtung! Achtung! Telephone call for Herr Dryer.' The voice seemed very like J. K. Lever's.

Don Topley was a medium-pace bowler in those days (His son Reece is now in the England set up). On one occasion Topley was bowling and Ray Julian was umpire. After a delivery Topley made his way back to his mark. He then ran back to the stumps. 'How many balls, Ray?' 'That's three, Don.' Topley got back to his mark again, then ran back to the umpire – 'Is that three to come, or three gone?'

151

Chapter 29

Sir Tom Finney

Left to Right – Jimmy Greaves, Mike Newlin and Sir Tom Finney. A superb lunch at the Queens Hotel in Leeds

There are very few people who go through a very long life without making an enemy or two. Tom Finney was one. I got to know him and his wife Elsie well in later life and he came to a number of my lunches. Much was made of him being the Preston plumber, and so he was for most of his adult life. However, it was as a footballer for just one club, Preston North End, that he was a legend – their best ever player and never booked, let alone sent off, either for club or on his many appearances for England. Right wing, left wing or indeed centre forward made no difference to Tom. If Stan Matthews played at number seven Tom would wear eleven and his teammates always admired the great man. Bill Shankly played with him, and always said until the day he died, that Tom was the best player of all time.

I had heard many tales about how the Preston chairman had turned down an offer from Italian club Palermo in the early 1950s. Tom did not mention it much in his speeches, preferring to talk of his love for P.N.E or playing for England. Once in Leeds we were having a coffee prior to the event and I had the chance to ask him if he really would have liked to play in Italy. He looked around and smiled. 'Of course I would' – he went on to say that he was offered £200 a week (he was then on a great deal less at Preston), a smart motor and a lovely villa. Elsie was right behind the idea. When the chairman called him into the office he told Tom of the offer from Palermo, did he want to go? Tom said he would consider it. 'If you do, Finney, remember Preston hold your registration and if you go you will never play in England again.' Tom did not go – he really did love Preston – but the world missed out on seeing the genius at work. He never mentioned it again. After Sir Tom passed away aged ninety-one in 2014, I expected the 'Italian Job' to be mentioned. It never was.

Tommy Docherty was another who played with Tom at Preston, before going on to a long management career. He once managed to use Tom to aid his financial position at the club. At the end of the season in those days, if the player was to be offered a new contract for the following season he would have to see the chairman to discuss terms. Tom was first in and when he came out the Doc collared him. 'How did you get on Tom?' 'I got £15 a week in the season and £12 in the summer.' Armed with this detail Doc went in and was offered £15 in the season but only £8 in the summer. 'But you've offered Finney £12 in the summer.' 'Yes, but Finney is a better player than you.' 'Aye, but not in the f****** summer he's not!'

It is not recorded whether he got his twelve quid, but he signed anyway.

Chapter 30

Sir Alex Ferguson

I first met Alex prior to the knighthood. My good friend Wilf McGuinness was working at Old Trafford on match days, entertaining the corporate guests and had got to know the 'Boss' very well and thought that he would do a few lunches for me. Our first event was at Chester Racecourse, a favourite venue for my events, and a place that Fergie loved for his other great passion – horse racing. Our lunch was not on a race day and a full house turned up to meet the two United legends. Wilf as ever wowed them and I admit to a little apprehension as I introduced Alex. No need to worry, Sir Alex was brilliant. Guests (and me) sat open-mouthed as he recounted how, in the early years, he was building the club but results were not good, and there was much media speculation that the dreaded sack was looming. He recalled, just before an FA Cup match with Nottingham Forest, that he got a call from the United chairman's secretary that Martin Edwards wanted to see him in his office. Fergie told us that he did think of clearing his desk, but resisted the temptation and went up to Mr Edwards's office. 'Sit down, Alex. You will be aware of the press speculation about your position. Well it is just speculation, your position is not under discussion. Now, I am going to be unavailable to anybody until Monday. So, go and get a win at Forest.' This Fergie did and the rest is history, United and football's greatest manager of all time.

When asked if there was a single player who had contributed to the great success, he again surprised everyone by saying that it was Eric Cantona. In those days, the team would train in the mornings at the Cliff training ground. At lunchtime, he said, you would not see the players for dust. Eric arrived from Leeds United and at the end of the session, the players were gone, but Cantona asked Fergie if he could have a couple of the youth team, who were training on the far side of the ground. So, Alex ran over to Eric Harrison, the youth team coach, and got a couple of lads. When he got back to Eric the Frenchman smiled and said, 'And a goalkeeper.' Alex said there might have been a swearword or two, but Cantona probably did not understand football language! Back he came with a keeper and Eric spent an hour volleying balls at the young goalie until finally calling it a day. Football is strange, Sir Alex told us. After training the following day, most of the players left as usual, with the exception of just one. Captain Bryan Robson was hanging around and watching the Cantona show. Within a week the United sessions had completely changed. Fergie gave the credit, not to himself or his coaching staff, but to the charismatic Frenchman.

As I write Manchester United have José Mourinho at the helm. If he struggles with results and fails to win over their fans or the press. I wonder if the current regime will stick with him as Martin Edwards did with Sir Alex? I tend to doubt it. It's strange to see the similarity between today and what happened to Wilf McGuinness when Matt Busby retired for the first time in 1970. I doubt that Sir Alex will be tempted out of retirement, I very much doubt it. Lord Fergie perhaps?

Chapter 31

Bob 'The Cat' Bevan, Bobby Moore and Me!

M B N   P R O M O T I O N S
present

A

Sporting

LUNCHEON

with

"The Great Goalkeepers"

Gordon Banks OBE, Pat Jennings,
Alex Stepney & Bob 'The Cat' Bevan

at the Hotel Piccadilly, Manchester
on Monday 14th March 1994

Sponsored by

GLF

GRUBER ~ LEVINSON ~ FRANKS
CHARTERED ACCOUNTANTS

I was a goalkeeper from a young age. I dreamt of emulating my Wolves hero Bert Williams. Despite unsuccessful tries at getting to West Ham and Leyton Orient with my good pal Gerry Cronin, we ended up at Southern League Romford, who were then managed by another international keeper, the former Spurs star Ted Ditchburn. Ted coached me, and quickly gave it up as a bad job. Gerry and I decided that our own side, on Sunday mornings, would be good. We soon became such a good side I couldn't get into the team! So, a different role seemed a better option and I managed Arroway Athletic for over ten years. We were coming to the notice of clubs in the Essex area, and John Dick, the West Ham and Scotland forward who was coaching West Ham's junior teams, encouraged me to do my FA coaching badge. But, as for many young men, there were lots of other attractions. I was acting in amateur drama, was courting a lovely girl at work (fifty years on we are still together, brave girl that Doreen) so I progressed my career in the building society world.

Move on several years and I was managing New Mills in the Cheshire League. Finance was a problem (as it is with most clubs) so I put together a sportsmen's dinner in Stockport to raise funds. My mentor Freddie Pye, then chairman at Wigan Athletic, came along and our guest speaker was to be Bob 'The Cat' Bevan, who introduced himself as the Old Wilsonians 6th XI goalkeeper. His opening line was that 'They call me the Cat, not because I was particularly lithe and athletic, being over sixteen stone, but I was once abused by a bloke called Tom.'

Bob was actually a brilliant stand-up comic, who had famously done a 'team talk' for Brighton and Hove Albion when they got to the FA Cup Final against Manchester United. They drew in the final, but lost the replay. We went on to do many events together. Just a taste of his unique speech was that Old Wilsonians were in an early season relegation battle with Fulham Council Old Boys on the local rec. They waited for ages for the referee to come out of the dressing room, so Bob went to see what the problem was. In the room was a very pretty woman, in full reffing outfit. 'Is there a problem Miss?' 'Yes. I am not coming out. There's a referee on the next pitch in the same outfit ...' Bob decided that flattery would be the best course of action: 'I say, you look lovely in those tight shorts, how do you get into them?' 'You could try gin and tonic,' was her reply! Anyway, she did emerge and was doing very well until, following a corner, disaster struck as the Old Wilsonians' captain added a whole new meaning to the previously known football term, banged it in the back of the net, after which the referee left the game, and the skipper went with her.

Bob said he had let in many hundreds of goals, in many ways, but that it would have been a lot fewer if his glasses had not steamed up, or got splashed on wet days.

Bob asked me if I would consider doing a series of my MBN lunches with the England World Cup winning captain Bobby Moore? What a silly question, would I! They were great. I had met Bobby at West Ham but did not know him. All the stories about him are well recorded, so all I can say was that he was a real professional and bounced well off the 'Cat'. They were watching a game at Upton Park one evening when Bobby enquired of 'The Cat', 'Cat, have you always been a custodian?' 'No, Mooro, in my younger years I was a tough tackling midfield ball player, not unlike yourself, but with a touch more skill and pace ...'

Our final lunch was in Birmingham and Bobby, Cat and I caught a train back to London. At the station Bobby was met by his daughter Pippa and before he left he said, 'Mike the lunches were great, can we do some more?' I said I would be delighted. But fate took its worst hand not long after and the great man was struck down by the dreaded cancer, how unfair.

After Bobby retired as a player he never made it in management. Harry Redknapp told me a lovely story. He got a call from Bobby to say that he was to be the new manager of Oxford and would Harry give him a hand and join him on the coaching side? 'There's not much money but it's a good opportunity.' Harry said OK and they drove to Oxford for a chat to the chairman. Harry was amazed when they arrived that they were not to be the new management team at Oxford United, but at lowly non-leaguers Oxford City.

Bob and I were great goalkeepers in our own minds. I thought that a great way to use the 'Cat' for some more lunches was to have a show called (admittedly not very original but appropriate), 'The Great Goalkeepers'. It became one of my best series of events, and Bob even pinched the idea and claimed in his autobiography that he had thought up the idea! Never trust a goalie!

Our first, and probably best event featured England's finest keeper of all time, Gordon Banks. He was joined by Northern Ireland's legend Pat Jennings, all held together by 'The Cat'.

Greatest is a word that appears many times in my book – sorry but sometimes it is the only word appropriate and 'Banksy' as 'Cat' called him, recalled 'that' save in World Cup 1970 against Brazil. 'The outside right, Jairzinho, crossed the ball, Pele leapt like a salmon and from six yards headed the ball goalwards, I dived to my right and somehow flipped the ball up and over the bar.' The Cat was never short of a word. 'Great save Banksy, but frankly I would have held it ...'

On another occasion Peter Bonetti, the Chelsea and England star, got the treatment when he asked Bob why he used the 'Cat' as it was *his* nickname around the world? 'To be honest, Pete, you only got that nickname because you could lick your own balls!' Bob was never really unkind to any of our guests, though – he always laughed with them not at them – so nobody turned down my requests to join the team. Gil Merrick, Ray Clemence, Bert Williams, Harry Gregg, Ronnie Simpson, Alan Rough, Bruce Grobelaar, Neville Southall, Peter Shilton – what a group!

I will finish the goalkeeper section with an event that Bob Bevan did not attend. One of Manchester City's 'greatest' (sorry) was Bert Trautmann. Bert had been a German paratrooper and first came to Britain as a prisoner of war. Whilst in a POW camp he was allowed to play for St Helens Town FC and after the war was spotted by Man City. He overcame much abuse to become a massive favourite at Maine Road, before breaking his neck in the 1956 Cup Final against Birmingham City. He went to live in Spain, but came back for my lunch to celebrate his eightieth birthday. What a reception he got. He was still loved in Manchester and signed autographs for almost the whole audience.

Chapter 32

Before MBN

Viv Allen, [marketing manager Manchester Evening News] Nick Sanders[World record round the world cyclist]and Mike Newlin[Manager of the Northern Rock Building Society, prior to MBN, with a lot more hair !!!]

My first coaching job in senior non-league football was in 1977. I joined Athenian League club Redhill in Surrey. My job was to manage the reserve team. We did well and I signed Ian Noyce, who had played as a junior for Fulham. He was a class above most of the lads, and quickly made the first team. Redhill were not doing well and the chairman phoned me at work. Would I consider taking over the first team as the manager, Eamon Mulligan, was to move on. I asked for time to discuss it with Doreen, but fate took a hand. The next call was my boss at Northern Rock, Ray Chapman, and would I go north to manage the Manchester office? I would have loved to have managed

Redhill, but the money would have been low, and with three girls and another baby on the way, the sensible decision was to head up the M6. So sadly, I said no to the football job, and in March 1978 we moved to Brooklands near Manchester. It turned out to be the best move we ever made. I managed Bramhall from the Mid-Cheshire League for a time, before Freddie Pye suggested that I should go to manage New Mills FC, a Premier Division club in the Cheshire League (later to be the Northern Premier), one step down from the Conference (now National league). Freddie spoke to David Fisher the New Mills chairman, who had just parted company with former Rochdale winger Brian Taylor, who had worked hard with no budget. It was March and relegation was certain – I had seven or eight games to perform a miracle. Despite some excellent results we went down, and I ended up with no players from the old regime. I worked pre-season to find players from the local area, and added some from around the Altrincham region.

I spoke to Fred Pye and he agreed to bring the Wigan Athletic first team to New Mills for a pre-season friendly. It was a Tuesday kick off, 6.30, so I picked up some players in Manchester, and got to the ground, which sits on the Derbyshire–Cheshire border, at about 5 o'clock. Waiting outside the ground was the Wigan Athletic team bus, Freddie the chairman, board members including Sir Bobby Charlton, and manager of the Latics Larry Lloyd, a formidable centre half at Nottingham Forest, Liverpool and England. The gates were locked but I had a set of keys. I quickly wished that I had not! When I got in I was met with the sight of a country meadow, not resembling a football pitch! I got Mr Fisher on the phone. 'Chairman, Wigan are here, Bobby Charlton is waiting, and Larry Lloyd looks as if he is going to eat me, what goes on?' 'The groundsman is on holiday in Blackpool. I tried to cut the grass with my hover mower ...' 'Well at least the lines have been marked.' 'Are you on your way?' 'Well, no, I have an important meeting,' and the line went dead. Well, dear reader, what would you do now? A knock on the door, it is our referee, top Football League official Arthur Robinson, whom I knew well. He saw my face and we walked out to inspect the 'Millers' pitch. 'Crikey it's not great [understatement of all time] but at least it's marked out properly.' I approached Lloyd who I did not know and his assistant, Fred Eyre, who I also knew well and they said the game could go on. I was relieved, and we got under way. We lost 3–0 to a Les Bradd hat-trick, but that wasn't the most memorable part of the evening. During the first half Kevin Shelton, the Wigan winger, who later moved to Nottingham Forest, raced down the flank and in front of the New Mills fans, went to cross the ball. As he did so he kicked an enormous clod of curly kale and missed the ball completely. Les Bradd would probably have headed in the weed, if he hadn't been laughing so much! At half time Larry Lloyd refused to take the team back into the away dressing room which he eloquently called a 'shit hole'. Before the second half started Fred Eyre came over to our dugout. He had laughed so much that he almost wet himself but suggested I did not attempt to shake hands with Larry at the end of the game. I took his advice.

I suppose I should have cut my losses and left but I wanted the job, and the Chairman promised that things would improve and he was going to find a budget to pay the players. Not a lot but at least a chance to get a few quality men. My first signing was 'Wyn the Leap' – yes really, Wyn Davies the former Newcastle, Manchester United and City centre forward and Wales legend. Now Wyn was past his best at forty or so and had dodgy knees, but it created a buzz in the local paper. Add to him I also signed Vic Halom who had starred for Sunderland in the famous FA Cup Final win over Leeds in 1973. Vic was thirty-four and looking for a new club. We played Conference side Matlock Town at their ground in the Derbyshire Senior Cup and got a very creditable 0–0 draw – unfortunately it contributed to Peter Swan, the Matlock manager, getting the push. But the dreaded David Fisher struck again. My 'budget' did not materialise and my hope of getting £35 a week for Vic, and asking him to join me as coach vanished as well. He joined Northwich Vics, and our slide down the table was inevitable.

I made a desperate effort to inspire my motley crew and before one home game, my team talk went something like, 'You are not New Mills today, you are Ipswich Town [who were top of Division One at the time].' I told each player who he was. Kevan Hawkins was Arnold Muhren, John Crompton our right back was to be Mick Mills, the Ipswich captain and England international. It seemed to go down well but they came in at half time 2–0 down! I got my tea cups ready and started on Crompton, who had given away one goal – he stopped me in my tracks. 'Don't blame me, gaffer. It was Mick Mills's fault!'

I was sad to leave the Millers but I ended up at my non-league love Altrincham. Over the years I ran the reserve team on a couple of occasions, set up the youth team and ran a centenary dinner. Jack Charlton and Duncan McKenzie spoke and we put £25,000 in the coffers. However, I have never officially admitted to one major foul up … I got Tommy Docherty to manage the club. I was doing a lunch in Leeds with the Doc and Leeds legend Bobby Collins. During lunch I asked Tommy if he was finished with management. He said that he would still like to do one more job. I suggested Altrincham, and he jumped at the idea. That night I spoke to our chairman, Gerry Berman, who got very excited at the idea, and the deal was soon done. We had parted with the manager before this happened by the way! So there we were when we made the official announcement, with the BBC and many other press and media representatives present. The Doc was asked, on television, why he had joined 'Alty' and he joked that it was OK because the physio's wife was ugly. Not only was this reference to his previous marital troubles a bit near the knuckle, he did not know that our veteran physio was a local legend, Geoff Warburton, who had been with the club forever – he even bought the kit for them at the end of WW2. Now Geoff's wife was a lovely lady and when he got home that afternoon he found himself locked out. 'Your manager said I was ugly.' Geoff was forgiven but Tommy Doc was never forgiven at Altrincham. He was a disaster, and an expensive one. Non-league was not for him.

The BBC's Garry Richardson used to tell a story about his village side – 'Who is your centre forward Garry?' 'Kevin Keegan.' 'Wow, is that the Kevin Keegan who starred for Liverpool, Southampton, Hamburg and England?' 'Same name but no, he's the local butcher.' 'What about the centre half?' 'Bobby Moore.' 'Not the West Ham, Fulham and England World Cup Captain?' 'No, he's the local plumber.' 'What about the manager?' 'Tommy Docherty.' 'What, Tommy Docherty, Chelsea, Rotherham, QPR twice, Aston Villa, Porto, Scotland, Manchester United, Derby County, Sydney Olympic, Preston, Wolves … and Altrincham?' 'Yes that's the bugger.'

Chapter 33

Some Other Shorts

Garry Richardson is another good friend. His BBC television and radio interviews are great and he was a good speaker at many of my lunches. We did a series of events with big Frank Bruno. Frank played up to his reputation for not being the brightest bulb in the lamp. He is a lovely man and always won over an audience. Garry played his part with sensitive interviews. Just a taste ...

'Frank, you have a detached retina?'

'Yes, Garry, we do now. We moved from a bungalow.'

You can never judge an audience. In Birmingham at the end of a lunch a woman came up to top table and laid into Garry, verbally not physically thank goodness. 'You are disgusting to take the mickey out on Frank. You are racist ...' Frank leaned over and laughed that famous laugh, 'Garry is my friend.' End of scene. She still wanted autographs!

We had very few disasters at my events, although Peter Wheeler, now CEO at Leicester Tigers, and one of the best hookers for England and the British Lions, almost committed manslaughter! At the end of a lunch in the Hotel Piccadilly in Manchester, we drew a business card from a top hat (my great way to increase my database). The winner got a rugby ball, signed by Peter, and on this occasion it was an accountant from Deloittes. He was sitting in the second row so Peter took the ball and as a good hooker threw it to the winner, but as a joke threw it 'squint'. It hit a glass chandelier and neatly lifted off a three-foot shard of glass, which fell on to the seat of Robyn White, the Bank of Scotland manager, who luckily was out for a pee. Peter's face went completely pale and he jokingly asked if there was a solicitor in the house. About twenty guests got out their business cards. It cost me a free table at the next event, but could have been the first, and only fatality at my lunches. 'Wheelbrace' never forgot it though he still spoke for me on many other occasions …

Remember Erica Roe? Peter told of her famous topless appearance at Twickenham in the match against Australia in 1982. England had not played well in the first half. In those days, the players did not go to the dressing room during the break and captain Bill Beaumont got the team in a huddle and was unleashing a roasting. As he spoke he realised that he was losing their attention. All eyes were looking past him to a point in front of the stand, from where a great roar was erupting. Billy was determined not to be distracted and look round but finally started shouting at his teammates. Peter said 'Sorry, captain, but there's a bloke over there with your arse on his chest!' Erica had an ample bosom but Billy had an even bigger backside! England did go on to win, if anyone remembers the rugby …

1980 had been a great Grand Slam year for Bill Beaumont and his lieutenant and scrum half was Steve Smith of Sale, who went on to captain England when Bill retired. 'Smithy' recalled how different it might have been. In the very tight game against Wales Steve should have cleared a ball in the corner, he failed and Wales scored, the Grand Slam was in severe danger. As the England players trooped under the posts for the conversion. Smithy was a forlorn and lonely figure on his haunches in the corner. Only one man made his way over to the distraught scrum half. If you watch it on the television, you will see Bill put his hand on Smithy's shoulder and say a consoling word. Did he hell! He called Steve a 'stupid c***!'

Luckily for Steve's career Dusty Hare kicked a penalty that won the match for England and made the historic Grand Slam possible.

On an earlier visit to Cardiff, when Wales were in their seventies pomp, the England team were staying at the Angel Hotel in Cardiff city centre. It was only a short walk to the Cardiff Arms Park, and Billy Beaumont and Smithy were on their way to the ground when they were approached by an obviously

England supporter. Smithy said, 'He had a deerstalker hat rammed on his head, and a shooting stick rammed up his bum.' 'Beaumont, jolly good luck today. May the best team win.' Bill turned to Smithy and said, 'I f****** hope not.' The best team did win.

Staying in the rugby world Dublin has always been a great place to go in the Five, or Six, Nations. Whilst the rugby was important, the *craic* and the Guinness played a vital role. One of my best pals in the game is the former Ireland and legendary Lions flanker Fergus Slattery. 'Slatts' starred in Willie John's historic tour to South Africa in 1974. He is one of the best raconteurs and told stories more than jokes but he did have several good 'gags', one of which has been pinched by rugby speakers for many years. Fergus was having a Guinness in the Burlington Hotel in Dublin before a Lions lunch with England's Jason Leonard and Scotland's Gavin Hastings. When the conversation got on to 'happy hours', Jason said of his local, the Dog and Duck in Twickenham, 'If you buy a pint, the landlord gives you a second free.' 'That's nothing,' said Gavin. 'At my local the Swinging Sporran in Edinburgh, you buy a pint, and they give you another pint and a whisky chaser free.' 'That's nothing boys' said Slatts, 'At Kitty O'Shea's happy hour in Dublin, when you go in they buy you a pint, then another, then a couple of shorts, then they take you out and you get laid!' 'Blimey did that happen to you, Slatts?' said Jason. 'Not me, boys, but it did happen to my sister.'

Jason was never a svelte figure, front row forwards rarely are, but he remembers a day at Lansdowne Road during the Six Nations. He was injured and needed attention. It was on the far side from the dugouts and Jason asked the referee to call the physio. As he lay in pain a clear Irish voice came out from the crowd near the stricken forward, 'Leonard, you fat bastard, you don't need a physio, you need a fecking midwife.' Everybody laughed, even Jason through gritted teeth.

It was me that might have needed medical attention at one of my lunches in Bristol. My guest of honour was the former Tottenham Hotspur captain and England defender Gary Mabbutt. We were waiting for the main course when Gary, who is type one diabetic, said he needed to administer his insulin injection. I told him that I would keep his lunch warm. 'You won't need to,' was his response, and with that he pulled his shirt from his trousers and injected the insulin into his side. He was fine but I nearly fainted!

In 1963 a whirlwind hit non-league Romford. I was training there and into the dressing room one Tuesday evening came Malcolm Allison. He had played for West Ham until tuberculosis caused him to lose a lung. After that he coached young players at the Hammers, including a young Bobby Moore, but then had drifted out of the game. Ted Ditchburn the Romford manager, persuaded him out of retirement for a final season. Big Mal despite only having one lung, had one of the loudest voices I had heard on a football pitch. At Clacton Town on New Year's Day it almost got him arrested! Clacton's ground was right next to the bus station and twenty minutes into the game, Romford's John Evans managed to miss an open goal from one yard out. What Mal called him would have made the Pope blush and his temper did not improve when Willie Clark scored for Clacton. Minutes later a police inspector walked on to the pitch and warned big Mal that if he did not moderate his language he would be arrested. Apparently two elderly ladies were waiting for a bus and took great exception to the language coming from the football ground.

Years later, at the end of his colourful (to say the least) career, Mal came to live in Altrincham, and his son David played for me at New Mills, a very quiet, polite lad, not like his dad! Mal came and spoke at a lunch in Manchester. He recalled his days with Crystal Palace in the early seventies, not the infamous episode of cavorting in the team bath with a porn actress, but how black players were coming into league football. He saw that the players were forming cliques and this was affecting team morale, so before an away game he called the players together in the dressing room and told them that he was very unhappy at the atmosphere around the team. 'From now on there are no blacks or whites at Palace, from now on you are all "greens". Now get on the team bus, light greens at the front and dark greens at the back!'

Chapter 34

Denis Law

Left to Right – Guest of the Life Association of Scotland, Denis Law and Mike Newlin.
Denis was speaking at his first ever event for MBN in Birmingham.

When Denis Law was signed by Huddersfield Town in 1956 he could easily have been mistaken for a schoolboy – and he was stick-thin and wore glasses for a bad squint. Many players then and in the subsequent eighteen years found to their cost that Law was a very tough character, with a mean streak. He rarely took a backward step and fell foul of referees on a variety of occasions. Bill Shankly was his manager at Huddersfield and wanted to take Denis with him when he left to manage Liverpool. Liverpool could not meet the transfer fee and Denis went to Manchester City. Denis held Shanks in great regard and recalled that, when he was a young player, Bill got the youngsters together to discuss the opposite sex. 'If you are thinking of getting married' – Denis was just a lad at the time – 'You must do what I did to Nessie.

On the day we married, on our way to our honeymoon, I took my new wife of a few hours to watch Crewe Reserves play Rochdale Reserves.' Law moved on from Manchester City to play in Italy for Torino, before Matt Busby signed Denis in 1962 and he became 'The King' of Old Trafford.' The Lawman was another name that stuck and Best, Law and Charlton went into club history.

After retirement Denis became an accomplished speaker and we did several events with George Best. But he was happiest on his own. When taxed on how many times he got himself sent off, he would often, with tongue firmly in cheek, plead mistaken identity or victimisation. He would recall after one altercation that he was summoned to attend an FA hearing in London. Sir Matt went with him by train and told Denis to let him do the talking. This he was happy to do and Sir Matt told the committee that the ref had misheard 'my player Mr Law'. 'He called the referee a coot.' They did not believe Sir Matt and banned Denis for three weeks. Two further sending offs followed and longer bans were imposed. 'However, every downside had an alternative outcome as every sending off was near December, 'so for three years I got Christmas at home in Aberdeen'.

Denis missed the England World Cup win in 1966. He had a long-term engagement for a game of golf with an English pal. He refused to let his opponent change the times of their duel and they were walking around Withington golf course as England won. He did not tell us if the two remained friends.

In 1968 another serious injury caused him to miss the European Cup win over Benfica but some of his teammates took the trophy into the hospital to show him. He was grateful, and although he never regained full fitness he played on until 1974.

For Scotland, he was one of their most popular strikers. It was a non-footballing incident that he recalled at our Glasgow lunch. The story of Jimmy Johnstone getting into trouble after a drinking session at Largs, before the 1974 World Cup, has been told many times. It was early morning when 'Jinky' ended up with other players on the beach at the Ayrshire resort. He went out in a rowing boat and was drifting out to sea, when the Coastguard was called out to rescue him. It made the front pages of the newspapers, and a press conference was called to explain things. Jinky asked Denis if he would attend, 'Just to give me moral support,' he said. Denis reluctantly agreed. When it came to Jimmy's chance to explain … he promptly told the world's press that Denis Law had made him do it! He survived, by the skin of his teeth, but did not play in any of the World Cup games.

Denis played in the famous game when Scotland lost 9–3 to England at Wembley Stadium in 1961. In goal for Scotland was Celtic keeper Frank Haffey, who had a nightmare, so bad that when he retired not long after the match, he decided to emigrate to Australia. Twenty years later Denis was on a speaking tour with Bestie and he ran into Frank in Sydney. 'Hello, Denis, can I come home yet?' he asked. 'Not yet, Frank, not yet,' was Denis's reply.

Chapter 35

Graham Gooch

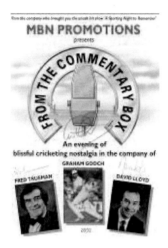

Front page from the tour brochure in January – March 1994 (26 nights from Torquay to Leeds)

Signing Autographs for some young fans

I've known Goochie for many years. Strangely I played cricket against his dad. I played for Anson St George at Grange Farm Sports ground in Chigwell. We played all day Sundays, and Alf played for East Ham Corinthians and a very young Graham got his love of the game from his much-loved dad. We met years later when he was England's greatest opening batsman and had a benefit season planned from Essex CCC. He had spoken at a few lunches for me, and as part of his testimonial year he asked me to organise some 'Evening with Graham Gooch' nights. We had good nights with former Glamorgan and England spinner Peter Walker, who had the role of interviewing Goochie.

My favourite story was about an Essex match against Somerset at the Taunton ground. Making his debut for Essex was Ian Pont, the younger brother of Essex regular Keith. Pont was a lively quickie but as yet, unknown. Goochie gave him the new ball and he got Peter Roebuck out early on. Walking in to bat next was Viv Richards, the great West Indian. Goochie was at slip and mentioned to fellow slipper Ken McEwan that Viv looked in a good mood so he hoped Pont would not upset the great man. Pont ran in and bowled a fierce bouncer that left Viv on the seat of his flannels, with Ian Pont staring at him. Viv dusted himself down and turned to Goochie, 'Who is this Ponty maan?' Pont was back at his mark and the next ball was delivered. Goochie said there were two 'gunshots' – the ball hitting Viv's bat, and then crashing into the advertising boards. 'Ken we're in for a long day,' was Goochie's reaction. Ian Pont went back to the end of his run up, and steamed in, Viv got ready for another bouncer, but Pont bowled a slow full-pitched ball that Viv tried to hit into Taunton. He nicked it, however, to the Essex wicket-keeper, David East. I. V. A. Richards c. East b. Pont 4. David East is a good pal, now running cricket in the UAE, and became the joint world-record-holder for catches by a keeper in an innings in that game – eight I think. As Viv walked back to the Pavilion, Pont was being congratulated by his teammates, when he turned to Keith Fletcher and enquired, 'Who was that young black chap?'

On a similar, and oft-told theme, Goochie recalled how a young Test quickie, Greg Thomas, had tried to rile the great Viv Richards. He bowled him a bouncer that whistled past the great man's nose. That would have been fine, but Thomas followed up with a 'sledge'. 'It's red and round and weighs five and a half ounces.' With that he stomped back to the end of his run up ready to steam in again. He pitched it half-way down the track, and Viv hit it out of the ground and spoke, for the only time in the game, 'You know what it looks like, go and find it.'

Shane Warne was Australia's greatest spin bowler. He came to a number of lunches with his friend Merv Hughes, and was always asked about 'that' ball, his first in an Ashes match. He pitched the delivery so wide outside the leg stump that batsman Mike Gatting let it go, only to see it turn so far that it knocked back his off stump. Shane always modest, said it was brilliant! Goochie, however, had another take on the subject. He used to say, 'It was a pity that Warnie didn't bowl a cheese roll at Gatts, as Gatts would definitely have eaten it.'

As a boy I had many happy years watching Essex play cricket. Goochie and David East became pals and I was able to help Trevor Bailey by introducing him to Chris Cowdrey, to auction some of his memorabilia, as we had done for Fred Trueman. I also played at Walthamstow CC and Essex played a game there, midweek, most years. Gooch, however, cost our club money. When he was eighteen he opened the batting on our ground, and proceeded to keep hitting our opening bowler, Dennis Sayers, into the builder's yard next door. We lost so many 'nuts' that it looked like the game might have to be abandoned. Anyway, Gooch got out before too long, though someone had popped down to the local sports shop just in case. I hope Essex paid for the replacements.

I am exactly the same age as the Essex president, who for many years was their premier off spin bowler, David Acfield. I was bowling off spin for Walthamstow and played against Acfield who was with Old Brentwoods. Our captain that day was

John Welch, who also ran the county second eleven. I was touched when I heard in the bar that he had compared me to David Acfield. 'Compared to Acfield, Newlin was crap ...' Unkind, but, sadly, more than a little true.

181

Chapter 36

Sir Terry Wogan

It's 31 January 2016, and I have just got up to hear about the passing of Sir Terry. I did not know him but was a loyal listener to his breakfast show on Radio 2 and countless other occasions that he made the world smile. Can I share just a few of my memories?

My first was driving to work in Croydon in the seventies. *Paint Your Wagon* was a popular film at the time and Lee Marvin had a hit record with a song from the film called 'Wandering Star'. Not musically very great, but Marvin could hit a very low note as he warbled 'wandrin, wandring staaaar'. Terry of course latched on to the record, and played it often. I was stopped at traffic lights in Purley as Lee reached the lowest note, Terry had encouraged us all to join in and as I reached 'star' I glanced at an old gentleman in the BMW next to me, he was in the same distress, and we laughed so much that the following cars were getting a bit annoyed. Never saw him again, wonder if he remembers?

When I settled 'up north' I was asked by the Duke of Westminster to assist the NSPCC in its centenary fundraising appeal. One of the events I planned was a rugby match between a Northern side with stars like Steve Smith, Tony Neary and many others and an Irish XV that Fergus Slattery had put together. He got almost a full international side, Moss Keane and the like, and we were playing at Broughton Park in Manchester. I wanted some publicity, so I dropped a note to Sir Terry telling him that Slatts was bringing the Ireland team to our game for the NSPCC, would he give it a mention? Imagine my surprise when he said, 'Now I've heard from my old friend Mike Newlin that Fergus Slattery will be at Broughton Park RFC on Sunday for an NSPCC charity match against the English. Go along and give the boys a cheer.' Wow, I was so chuffed. I'm now Terry Wogan's old pal. What I didn't realise was that Broughton Park Rugby Club were not prepared for the flood of phone calls about the game. In the end over 2,000 filled the ground thanks to the great Sir Terry.

Years later my PGA Annual Christmas lunch at the Grosvenor House had become part of the London calendar, and still is today thanks to Sandy Jones at the PGA and is run by my daughter Lisa of PT Events. I wanted to get Sir Terry to attend, and receive a recognition of his love of golf. So I spoke to Peter Alliss, who though it a great idea, as did Sandy, and it happened in 2008 with 1,100 guests. To my sadness, as I had to miss the event, so I never got to meet the great man.

Chapter 37

Some More 'Faces'

Left to Right – Comedian Brendan Healey, Mike Newlin and Sir Bobby Robson

I had the greatest job in the world. I met many of the most famous people in sport, and the happy audiences they addressed meant that very few of my events would have been considered not up to standard. Those that failed I would never mention. Everybody wants to entertain but not all can be a success. However, I am going to finish my trip down memory lane with some of the speakers who have been part of my life and essential to the success that made MBN Promotions the leading suppliers of corporate hospitality. I always said that if you did not like laughing, don't waste your money by attending.

Duncan McKenzie is a freak of nature! Not only was he a brilliant footballer but he could probably have played cricket at the highest level, and could hit a golf ball for miles. He had a relatively slim frame but was a class centre forward – he is in Everton's Hall of Fame, and at Leeds United he once famously jumped over a Mini car, so I guess he might probably have been an Olympic high jumper as well. Add the fact that he could throw a cricket ball further than most and you can possibly add shot put to the list. Apart from always losing money to him on the golf course, I admire Duncan as one of the best speakers – he graced countless events for me. He loved Brian Clough, who took him to Leeds from Nottingham Forest, though Cloughy promptly got sacked after forty-four days, falling out with the Leeds stars of the time. Duncan stayed for a couple of years and won over that tough crowd at Elland Road before moving to Goodison Park, where he still entertains guests at home matches.

Kevin Connelly is the best impressionist I have ever worked with. A bold statement, but though McGowan, Culshaw and the rest are good, Kevin is better! This, of course, is only my opinion, forged from listening to him at even more lunches than with Duncan McKenzie. He did not tell jokes he did not need to. At one lunch one of the guests told me that he had done thirty-two voices, and he knew them all. At the next event, I closed my eyes and he beat the record with thirty-three, and I knew every one. Big Jack, Greavesy, Johnners, Goochie, Bobby Robson, the list was endless. It gave me an idea – we were preparing an event in memory of Johnners, and Kevin and I were discussing how he could mark what was a sad, but happy occasion. As ever with Kevin, he started to go through his non-sporting repertoire and gave me a rendition of Noel Coward singing 'Can you please provide us with a Bren gun' – surreal but true. I asked him to do Groucho Marx and this gave me an idea. Just imagine the Grosvenor House at the 'Memories of Johnners' lunch. Down from the roof comes that famous voice, 'Hello everyone, Johnners here. Guess what? They play cricket in heaven. Noel Coward is captain of course and he's setting the field. Groucho come in to gulley,' and so on, all in those voices. We laughed for hours. He did it on the day. Barmy but true, and a lovely memory, I know Johnners would have approved. We also had the joy of getting Sir Bobby Robson to a lunch before we lost him. Kevin did a brilliant Sir Bobby, ever so gently taking the mickey out of Bob's occasional malapropism: 'I enjoyed managing in Holland, and spoke fluent Hollish. PVC were a good team. However, my business attempt was not good, there's not much call for a mountain bike shop in the Netherlands.' Kevin did not do that bit at our lunch, I wonder why?

Sir Bobby Robson was another gentleman of sport. We only got a couple of events together, the first one being at the Queen's Hotel in Leeds, where he entertained a sell-out audience. The affection in the room was so overwhelming you could almost touch it. However, Kevin Connelly and I laughed so much because the great man gave us a 'classic'. Bobby stood up and recounted 'My father was a miner. It was a really hard life – just imagine having to work at 2,000 feet *above* sea level.'

Chapter 38

The Female of the Speakers

Left to Right, Rachael Heyhoe-Flint, Mike Newlin and Frances Edmonds

At my first event at the Brahms and Liszt pub in 1980 there was only one woman in the audience. Shan Spencer is a much-respected lawyer in Manchester, who has had a great career in corporate recovery. She loved the lunches and for many years sponsored my Christmas event in the Hotel Piccadilly. I was never keen on raffles or auctions of memorabilia in the early years, but Shan persuaded me to do a collection for her favourite charity, Childline. We raised many thousands at the festive events. As the years passed the percentage of women attending grew, and whilst one or two of my speakers became nervous of causing offence with football language, they had no need to worry, the women enjoyed the stories – as long as they were good!

Getting female speakers was a totally different problem. I tried hard, but it was not easy. My first success was Rachael Heyhoe-Flint, now Baroness but then just 'Flintlock' as Frances Edmonds called her. Rachael was the England Women's cricket captain and went on to become the first female full member of the MCC. Not unused to dealing with all-male and occasionally inebriated audiences, she was a superb and entertaining speaker. At one Manchester event a guest, I think genuinely, asked Rachael if she wore a protective box when she batted. 'Of course I do, but I call it a manhole cover!'

On a cricket theme, Frances Edmonds – distinguished author, TV personality and wife of Middlesex and England spinner Phil Edmonds, was a great pal of Flintlock and we did a few 'women on top' lunches. At one she amazed the crowd as she talked about a long-gone boyfriend 'He thought he was the world's greatest lover … until he found out that I had asthma.'

The list is sparse but Dame Mary Peters was a wonderful guest of honour. We did a lovely lunch in her home town of Belfast and again in the Grosvenor House in London. She was a good friend of the legendary rugby star Cliff Morgan, who was another regular speaker for me.

One who got away was Sue Barker. Ian Robertson said that she was considering speaking, as she was not sure where her presenting career (then with Sky) was going. So, we had lunch at the Grosvenor House and she told me some lovely stories about her life in tennis. She was not fond of Ilie Nastase, who had been rude to her – how can anyone be rude to Sue Barker? And she went on to tell a racy tale of playing with the great Aussie John Newcombe. This would make a fantastic base for a speech I told her. As lunch finished she dropped what became a bombshell. She had just received a call from the BBC to ask if she would consider being the new host of *A Question of Sport*. Dammit – what could anyone say but 'Go for it.' She did and the rest is history. We did not get a speaker but we all got one of the best presenters of the age.

My only other regret was that I never got Victoria Wood to speak. Just imagine the ballad of Barry and Freda at an MBN lunch. Another of the best talents to leave us prematurely in 2016.

Chapter 39

How It All Started

What an exciting day. We have never won the World Cup, and here we are at the home of football and only West Germany, not even the whole of Germany, can stop us ruling the world! I have just gone into the tunnel at Wembley, when I see Les Cocker hurrying towards me. 'Mickey,' (that's what they call me) I prefer Mike, but that's the game, so Mickey it is. 'Mickey, Alf wants you in the dressing room, now'. So, in I go. All the boys are there, in various stages of undress, the game is not far away. 'Mickey what's it like out there?' asked Nobby. He looks nervous; he is in just a jock strap and his eyes are very red, I think he must be crying, but Jack says he has just put his contact lenses in. 'Have you seen them, kidder, they're like bottle tops!' Alf Ramsey calls me over, 'Michael, Robert is unable to play so I want you to replace him.' Does he mean our captain or is it Bobby Charlton? I look round the room, Bobby Moore is still in his kit, boy he looks like a blond James Bond, can't be him, so it must be Bobby Charlton.

'Now, Michael, the Germans have one star player. He is called Franz Beckenbauer, I would like you to mark him. Do not let him out of your sight for the whole ninety minutes. Have you anything to say?' 'No, Mr Ramsey. I mean yes, Alf, he won't get a kick, do you want me to kick him?' 'No, no, no, if I wanted him kicked I would have asked Norbert.' That was it. I am sitting next to Roger, from Liverpool, and can hardly tie up my Adidas boots. I pull on the red shirt with the three lions, and wonder why we are playing in red, whilst the Germans are in white? A bell rings and Bobby Moore gets up, 'OK let's go and win that cup.'

The roar as we emerge from the tunnel engulfs us. We look up at the twin towers and then I look for my girlfriend and mum and dad in the crowd – no chance of seeing them! I do see Franz leading the Germans, but seeing Nobby and Bally, who have to look after midfield, gives me confidence. We are under way. Alf's instructions are ringing in my head. Where's Franz? No need to worry – he's marking *me*. Suddenly the Germans cross the ball from their left wing, Ray Wilson heads it back into our box, and Helmut Haller scores. We are 1–0 down. Don't panic Mike! We get a free kick thirty yards out on our left wing. Our skipper steps up and a great diagonal cross finds his West Ham teammate Geoff Hurst, and just as he had done to the Argentinians, Hursty buries a great header, one-all. Half-time comes, Alf looks as cool as a cucumber, and urges us to keep playing, we will win the World Cup.

Bobby comes up to me, 'When we win this Mickey come and have a pint in the Retreat lunchtime tomorrow.' 'Will do, captain.' The Retreat pub in Lambourne End is a Hammers haunt, Bob lived on Manor Road, Chigwell, and I lived on Arrowsmith Road, Chigwell. As the second half goes on the Hammers factor increases as Martin whacks in our second goal. Now, we believe, the end of the game is close. Then Big Jack gives away a free kick just outside our box, it looks a dodgy decision – Jack thought so and the language coming from the big Geordie is ripe. The Germans get the ball into our six-yard area, and Weber scores from close range: 2–2. The final whistle blows. I think Jack is going to explode, but we make our way to the centre circle. Alf tells us to stand up. 'Don't show them you are tired. You have won this game once, now go out and win it again.'

Nobby comes up to me, 'Mickey, when we win this game, get my teeth. They're in a handkerchief in Callie's pocket, I can't meet the Queen without them.' We didn't know that our third goal will cause controversy for years. Alan Ball races down the right wing and catches Nobby's pass, I don't know what gives Bally his energy but I wish I had some. His cross finds Hursty, who smacks it against the bar, and it bounces down at least a yard over the line. (It did. I ask Roger if it was 'over the line' and 'miles over' is his reply). Mr Dienst, the Swiss referee, goes over to his Russian linesman, who points to the centre – goal! We are 3–2 up. In the second half of extra time we stay in front. Seconds from the end the Germans break on their right wing, and hit a dangerous cross into our six-yard box. Our brilliant captain reads it, and with big Jack yelling at him to kick the ball over the stand, Bobby passes to Bally on the edge of our area, and promptly gets the return back. With Jack about to have a heart attack, Bob glides between two opponents and hits a great ball over Hursty's shoulder. Geoff runs on and blasts a shot into the top corner of Hans Tilkowski's net. Jack comes up to me, 'Mickey, I'll never be able to play this effing game.' The final whistle goes, but Gawd I've forgotten to get Nobby's teeth!

*

'Are you ever going to get up?'

I find I am in bed at 57 Arrowsmith Road, Chigwell, Essex. It's actually Hainault, but Chigwell is the postal area, and is much posher. It's Sunday 31 July 1966. I don't suppose today of all days Bobby and the West Ham boys are *really* going to the Retreat? Anyway, I think I'll go for a pint, just in case.